Digital creativity

OWEN KELLY

Owen Kelly is an artist, writer and lecturer. He is
currently course tutor for multimedia at
Lambeth College in south London. He can be
reached at owen@booha.demon.co.uk

Published by Calouste Gulbenkian Foundation,
London 1996

Published by the Calouste Gulbenkian Foundation
98 Portland Place
London
W1N 4ET
Tel: 0171 636 5313

© 1996 Calouste Gulbenkian Foundation

ISBN 0 903319 73 X

British Library Cataloguing-in-Publication Data
A catalogue record for this book is available from the British Library

Cover design by Chris Hyde
Text design by Susan Clarke for Expression
Printed by Expression Printers Ltd, London N5 1JT
Distribution by Turnaround Publisher Services Ltd,
27 Horsell Road, London N5 1XL; telephone 0171 609 7836

You can't make footprints in the
sands of time by sitting down
Larry Norman

Contents

Tools & protocols

1 Computers and computing *15*

2 Media and multimedia *19*

3 The nature of multimedia *22*

4 Computers and protocol *26*

5 Performance and MIDI *29*

6 Text and the Internet *33*

7 Hypertext and the web *36*

8 The road to Nowhere *40*

Footprints in the sand

9 Prefabricated melody *47*

10 Musically alive environments *53*

11 The composer dances *57*

12 Sculpting in No-D *62*

13 Painting by numbers *67*

14 Creative experiences in virtual galleries *73*

15 Digital experiences in the real world *77*

16 Bits of language *82*

17 No paper please, we're digital *87*

18 A screen is not a page *93*

19 Learning digitally *97*

Digital creativity

20 State of the art *105*

21 The information dirt-track *109*

22 Build it and they will come *112*

23 The world tomorrow *115*

Index *128*

Acknowledgments

Digital Creativity was commissioned by Fiona Ellis when she was Assistant Director, Arts, of the Calouste Gulbenkian Foundation UK Branch. I would like to thank Fiona for her encouragement and endless enthusiasm and Ben Whitaker at the Foundation for his support in seeing the project through.

Denny Robson had the unenviable job of editing the manuscript, and I am indebted to her. The book is considerably better for her involvement, and I am profoundly grateful for the time and energy she brought to it.

I would like to thank everyone who agreed to be interviewed, or spend time with me, during my research; and all those who agreed to read the many and various drafts. In particular I would like to thank Russell Southwood, whose detailed critique was invaluable in the final stages of writing.

Despite the extraordinary help I have received from a large number of people, the responsibility for the book is mine and any errors, omissions or misunderstandings should be laid at my door alone.

Finally I would like to thank my son Jack, for allowing himself to be taken to see various events which were not exactly high on his personal list of priorities.

Owen Kelly
April 1996

Foreword

When this book was first commissioned computers were better understood by six year olds than by forty-six year olds. The Internet was the province of anoraky enthusiasts with pale skin and bad eyesight. Platforms were something you stood on waiting vainly for trains.

This was only just over a year ago. Now at the corner of Stamford Hill and Manor Road there is a billboard advertising the Internet service provider Demon to the not particularly rich or technically-minded folk of Stoke Newington.

At this year's conference of the Association of British Orchestras the City of Birmingham Symphony Orchestra's website was described to a substantial audience, who seemed to understand what was being said to them. On-line newspapers are readily available to anyone with equipment costing less than the price of a Continental holiday for a family of four.

Speed like this is frightening ... and exciting. The computer on which I am writing this does not even recognise the word 'Internet', so the spellchecker keeps pulling me up!

The 'message' of this book has changed. Once it was to have been a gentle introduction to the magic world of computers for artists too wary to take the plunge. Now it is altogether more urgent.

If words and phrases such as 'hypertext', 'sampling', 'digitising' or 'website' mean little to you, then you should read this publication now ... especially if you are an artist.

If you know what these words mean, but think they do not affect you, then you should read this publication now ... especially if you are an artist.

If you had hoped that none of this computer nonsense would happen in your lifetime, then you should read this publication now ... especially if you are an artist.

Digital Creativity also has a plea attached.

Time was (not very long ago) when computers seemed to threaten much that was familiar, including tools of artistic creation and means of artistic communication – bad shorthand for things like 'paint', 'keyboards', 'concerts' and 'books'. That remains true up to a point. But what is also true is that if the digital world described in the book is not to be culturally barren or embarrassingly anodyne then it needs artists to colour it, to give it life and body, music and language.

So, especially if you are an artist, please do not abandon this space to those with little to say or limited imagination.

Fiona Ellis
formerly Assistant Director (Arts)
Calouste Gulbenkian Foundation UK Branch
April 1996

Introduction

The industrial revolution has run out of steam and the mechanical age is winding down. We are witnessing the beginnings of a digital revolution: a major technical and cultural shift which will usher in the information age.

Or so we are told.

As long ago as 1980 Alvin Toffler claimed that the world was on the verge of The Third Wave, in which agriculture and industry would be superseded by information as the driving force in society. In 1995 Nicholas Negroponte, the founder and director of the Massachusetts Institute of Technology's Media Lab, confidently predicted that soon, for most purposes, 'atoms will be replaced by bits'. It is not necessary to be completely convinced by the technological optimists to recognise that something is going on. We can read about it on a daily basis in the media, and we can see it in the high streets.

On 15 November 1994 the *Daily Telegraph* launched *Electronic Telegraph*,[1] a professionally created daily electronic version of the newspaper which was (and is) made available free on the Internet. Since then the *Times*, as well as *New Scientist*, *Time Out*, and a host of other magazines, have developed on-line cousins. Some are simply digital versions of the printed item, while others like the *Guardian*'s GO2 and the *Daily Mail*'s SoccerNet are more customised. In this same period, the leading magazine publishers in Britain have all launched regular titles devoted solely to the wonders of the Internet.

Meanwhile, the shelves of newsagents are currently awash with magazines containing 'free' CD-Roms mounted on the cover – and not all of them are computer magazines. Even the Rolling Stones' latest compact disc *Stripped* contains an extra three video tracks that can be played on a PC or Macintosh equipped with a CD-Rom player.

Under Al Gore's leadership the US government has begun championing efforts to construct a National Information Infrastructure – the so-called information superhighway. In Britain Tony Blair has attempted to follow suit by negotiating with BT and publicly promising[2] that every school and community centre will be given free access to the Internet.

However, although the much-heralded digital revolution might finally appear to be underway, there are still real doubts as to whether or not it *is* a revolution, or whether it is merely another much-hyped fad like CB radio, the F-Plan diet, baseball caps worn backwards or body piercing.

According to the evangelists and enthusiasts the digital revolution is the beginning of the next stage in human evolution, and it is destined to change the way we live in the twenty-first century at least as much as the industrial revolution changed the way life was lived in the nineteenth and twentieth centuries. For many others, though, talk of ROM and RAM, of multimedia and cyberspace, of CD-Roms and the Web, is at best confusing or baffling – and at worst downright worrying. Some people feel that they do not understand it, some that they can never understand it, and many that they don't like what they do understand about it.

Digital Creativity is intended to address some of these concerns, as they affect 'new technology' and the arts. The book is concerned with the opportunities that computers and digital technology can provide for artists, educators, librarians and other cultural workers. It is also concerned with the likely effects of incorporating digital technology into the arts: on the means of production, the means of distribution and, ultimately, on the creative imagination itself. It is not therefore primarily concerned with the broader social, political and economic issues raised by the digital revolution, although I recognise that these are undoubtedly matters of great concern.

For the purposes of *Digital Creativity* I am defining 'the arts' very generally. I am taking them to mean any creative activity which is intended to entertain, provide pleasure, stimulate emotion or provoke thought. I am not differentiating here between those activities which are funded by the state, state agencies such as the Arts Council or the Regional Arts Boards, or philanthropic foundations, and those which are produced and distributed by commercial companies with the intention of making a profit.[3]

As this book demonstrates, the distinctions between different 'art forms', and between 'commercial' and 'non-commercial' work, are becoming very fuzzy in the digital realm. Phrases such as 'new technology' or 'multimedia' are used to describe work which bridges genres, blurs styles, and renders many traditional distinctions meaningless. For the purposes of *Digital Creativity*, the term 'multimedia' is therefore used in a very general way to describe a whole range of different work, from performance pieces which make use of computers, to hypertext and so-called expanded books, to websites and on-line soap operas.

Digital Creativity is in three sections. These provide, in turn, a brief guide to the background of the so-called digital revolution; a lengthier look at the creative uses to which digital technology is being put; and an overview of some of the likely consequences and developments of this activity. The book is aimed at a wide readership, some of whom may already be familiar with some of the topics that are addressed. For this reason, although each section refers back to material discussed in previous sections, the sections are more or less autonomous.

This book focuses primarily on work taking place in Britain, and much of the work discussed has been created in Britain. However, as Timothy Leary has said, 'distance has no meaning in cyberspace'. Using the Internet, it is as easy to communicate with California as with Cumberland, and as easy to work jointly on a project with someone in Berlin as with someone in Birmingham. For this reason, and because much of the pioneering work in the digital media was carried out in the USA and Europe, I make no apology for the frequent references to examples of comparable work from America, mainland Europe and elsewhere.

The examples used in the book are not restricted to work which is currently believed to be at the leading edge. They are taken from almost every decade this century. This is because, although the equipment being used to create 'multimedia' may be new and different, the ideas that are fuelling digital exploration have a complex history. They are related to, and drawn from, long-standing creative traditions in European, American, Eastern and African culture.

If we are at the beginning of a digital revolution, its consequences are going to be felt by people and not by machines. The major changes that occur as the result of a digital revolution will be cultural and not simply technological. This, then, is not a book about computers. It is a book about people attempting to use powerful tools creatively.

Digital Creativity is also intended as an invitation for other people to join them.

Tools and protocols

'Science is an edged tool, with which men play like children, and cut their own fingers.'

Sir Arthur Eddington

1 *Computers and computing*

The age of computing began in 1833. Alternatively, and equally plausibly, the age of computing can be said to have begun in 1946.

In 1833 Charles Babbage proposed an Analytical Engine. He envisaged a series of thousands of cogs and gear wheels which would carry out arithmetical functions. They would be programmed by inserting punched cards.[4] In 1841 a paper by the mathematician Ada, Lady Lovelace, persuaded the government to fund Babbage to develop what was now known as the Difference Machine. Unfortunately, the mechanics of the machine proved too complex to be practicable, and it was never built within Babbage's lifetime. For over a century it remained nothing more than an interesting idea.

In 1946, the US War Department announced an 'extremely sophisticated' calculator known as the Electronic Numerical Integrator and Computer – ENIAC – which was claimed to work over a thousand times faster than any other calculator. It used 18,000 vacuum tubes, and contained no moving mechanical parts. This machine was produced by International Business Machines, and convincingly demonstrated the advantage of moving from mechanical switches to electronic pulses as the basis of computation. It was arguably the first practical computer, in the sense in which we usually understand the term.

Throughout the 1950s there was a growth in huge computers which cost millions of dollars, took up entire rooms, and had to be kept at constant temperatures. They were maintained by specially trained engineers, and had neither screens nor keyboards. Instead, scientists wishing to use them took their stack of punched cards to have them fed into the machine by technicians who became known as the 'priests', and had their results returned to them on rolls of print-out paper.

In 1960 a new company called the Digital Equipment Corporation produced a smaller computer with a keyboard and screen, called the PDP1. This introduced what was then termed 'interactive computing', in which one person could work with the machine without the need for any intermediaries. It enabled the user to interact with the machine directly, without invoking any priestly help.

In 1974 the Xerox Corporation moved into computing and established its Palo Alto research centre, Xerox PARC. There a hand-picked team began building the kind of computer that they thought they would wish to use themselves. It was during the work carried out here that almost all the common metaphors of graphical, desktop-based computing were developed. Windows, icons, menus and pointers which changed as they were moved over different areas of the screen: all these originated at Xerox PARC. The first computer that the team produced was known as the Alto. It had 64k of memory, a mouse, and a high-resolution screen. It cost over $7,000.

In January 1975 the beginning of personal computing was announced by a cover story in *Popular Electronics*, describing the Altair 8800, a computer available in kit form from a tiny electronics company in New Mexico. Although the Altair 8800 contained so little memory and computing power that it was almost useless, it was nonetheless instrumental in sparking off interest in personal computing among a wide range of young scientists and engineers. These included Steven Jobs and Stephen Wozniak, the founders of Apple.

Since 1975 personal computers have come to seem essential for many businesses, colleges, hospitals, libraries and schools. In part this is because people have begun to understand how productive their use can be, but mainly it is because they have become cheaper, yet more powerful, year by year. In 1985, for example, an Apple Macintosh offering one megabyte of memory, a nine-inch black and white screen, and a floppy disk drive holding 800k disks, cost about £2,000. In 1995, much faster Macintoshes with eight megabytes of memory, fifteen-inch full colour screens, a floppy disk drive capable of using 1.5 megabyte disks, an internal 350 megabyte hard disk, *and* a CD-Rom drive were being sold for £1,200 or less.

These computers, though, however powerful their specifications, however sleek their casing, and however clever their marketing, are still essentially sophisticated calculators that store and manipulate very large amounts of binary numbers. They are still fundamentally 'stupid'. They do only what is asked of them and they do it completely literally, while performing up to several million instructions per second. It is this – the sheer volume of calculations that they are able to perform in any given time – that can make them appear to be acting semi-intelligently.

Cogent arguments have been advanced to suggest that computer stupidity is probably a temporary phenomenon, and that one day soon computers will achieve a kind of genuine intelligence, and with it an unknowable degree of autonomy. Kevin Kelly argues this in his book *Out of Control: the new biology of machines*, although he makes clear that in his opinion 'artificial intelligence, when it comes, will be intelligent but not very human-like'.[5] He suggests that many types of complex problem can be solved only by constructing computer programs that evolve and mutate, producing solutions that human programmers either had not, or possibly could not, have imagined.

Out of Control is based upon considerable research including guided tours of advanced research facilities. From this, Kelly produces arguments to suggest that a parallel, but genuine, kind of intelligence will emerge from technology when it is encouraged to evolve. 'When the Technos is enlivened by Bios we get artefacts that can adapt, learn and evolve. When our technology adapts, learns and evolves then we will have a neo-biological civilization.'[6] Not surprisingly, he argues that this will have profound social effects.

Kevin Kelly, and many others, predict a future in which our environment responds directly to our needs: in which rooms 'know' when to heat themselves and respond on their own initiative to verbal and visual cues, and automobiles automatically check to see whether they are a safe distance behind the car in front and adjust their speed, overruling the whims of the driver if necessary.

The likelihood of such predictions coming true, and the nature of the political and social changes that might be precipitated if they do come true, are outside the scope of this book. However, two of Kelly's conclusions are of direct relevance to the arguments being advanced here.

Firstly, it is important to point out that Kelly does not envisage a world of anthropomorphic robots acting in a pseudo-human manner. He does not predict the imminent arrival of Robby the Robot, and nor does he foresee the kind of future that Philip K Dick imagined in books like *Do Androids Dream of Electric Sheep?* Secondly, he believes that 'despite the increasing technization of our world, organic life – both wild and domesticated – will continue to be the prime infrastructure of human experience on the global scale'.[7]

In other words, no matter how intelligent computers seem likely to become, even those who are predicting (and advocating) an increasingly important role for them in our lives acknowledge that, for the foreseeable future, they are going to remain tools. Computers will not become humanoid, and they will not replace, intimidate or impersonate our friends (or our enemies).

Moreover, like all sensibly designed machines, computers will continue to have an off switch.

2 *Media and multimedia*

In approximately 1452 the book *Speculum Nostrae Salutis* was printed by Laurens Kostner. In 1454 Johann Gutenberg printed a copy of the Bible. Together these signalled the beginning of the age of movable type in Europe.

The age of the mass media, however, did not start until the industrial revolution. It started with the removal of stamp duty on newspapers in 1855, and the subsequent development of cheap periodicals and magazines. It was not until the first decade of the twentieth century, though, that the modern mass media really began. The launch of the *Daily Mirror* as a 'women's paper' was a turning point in the history of the press. The *Mirror* was the first newspaper regularly to print over one million copies, and the first to feature photographs regularly. Hitherto, illustrations had usually been provided by artists sketching or working with wood engravings or sometimes lithographs.

The launch of the *Daily Mirror* was made possible by a technological development: the invention – generally credited to Ira Rubel – of offset litho printing presses which were capable of printing large numbers of copies of a paper quickly and to a reasonable standard. Importantly, what was suddenly technologically possible dovetailed with what appeared likely to prove financially and politically profitable.

The development of cheap, mass-marketed newspapers and magazines was followed rapidly by the introduction of radio and television broadcasting. In 1920 KDKA became the world's first licensed radio station, transmitting from Pittsburgh Pennsylvania. KDKA was a commercial station, owned by Westinghouse. On 14 November 1922 the BBC began regular daily radio broadcasts from London. These, in contrast, were financed from the public purse. By 1929 the BBC was experimenting with television broadcasts, and in 1936 it began the world's first daily public television service.

This period saw the beginning of the mass distribution of recorded music on 78s, and in 1927 AMI Corporation introduced the first viable jukebox with electrical amplification and a choice of eight records.

This was also the period in which the commercial film industry was established. Within less than thirty years the silent film industry had risen to become a major cultural phenomenon and was then eclipsed by the introduction of talking pictures. The first talking picture, *The Jazz Singer*, was produced in 1926.

Cinema was marketed as a mass spectacle, with Hollywood rapidly assuming a mythic status as the world's dream factory. From the outset film stars were created and portrayed as distant, almost magical figures. Charlie Chaplin, Mary Pickford and many others became international celebrities, known to their public through the stories written about them in the mass circulation magazines.

The growth of the mass media was a process of continuing centralisation. The importance of the local newspaper was slowly eroded by the burgeoning national press, and subsequently by television. Local newspapers went from being a primary source of important news, through being a very secondary source, to being what they are today – primarily places to spot jumble sales and cheap second-hand cars.

During this period, then, the production of culture was industrialised and the primary focus of cultural life was inverted. However, while the most visible areas of cultural production became centralised, there were other strands of the industrialised media which seemed to be developing along different lines.

By 1910, for example, there were over seven million telephones in use in the USA. In 1912 the Post Office took over control of telephone communications in Britain, and the first automatic telephone exchange was opened at Epsom. By 1915 London and Birmingham had been connected by underground telephone lines, and the beginnings of a national service were established. Fifty years later, the satellite Early Bird was placed in a geostationary orbit over the Atlantic in order to relay transatlantic telephone calls.

From the outset telephones were deemed to be 'common carriers', mechanisms which relayed conversations over long distances with no editorial control. Telephones were not licensed and, in principle, anybody with access to a telephone could say anything they liked to anybody else with access to a telephone.

During the 1950s and 1960s the telephone moved from being primarily a business implement to become a standard feature of most homes.

Throughout this growth the telephone remained an interactive medium in which communication was two-way. Tapping phone lines and monitoring calls is still (officially) illegal without a court order.

In the last few years a number of international corporations have suggested that there will shortly be a convergence of the various information and entertainment media. They argue that televisions, video recorders, record players, home computers and telephones will soon be replaced by a single desktop set capable of carrying out all these functions and many more. This set will allegedly harness the digital power of computing in order to connect the user globally through enhanced telephone or television cables.

Supposedly, this kind of multimedia experience will return some sort of interactivity to daily cultural life. Viewers, listeners and readers will cease to be the passive recipients of centralised broadcasts and texts. They will become active participants – making choices that help determine the events of which they are a part, roaming a cornucopia of digital landscapes as they please, and adding their own contributions as they see fit.

The extent to which these suppositions prove to be true depends, of course, on the precise nature of the multimedia experiences that will be offered, and the ease (or lack of ease) with which people will be able to create their own.

Currently, there are a number of important limitations to the development of work in the digital media. At the time of writing, it is not possible to display convincing full-screen movies on a PC or a Macintosh, for example, because neither computer is capable of transferring sufficient information from a storage device to the screen at the speed necessary to generate the illusion of full-screen moving images.[8]

3 *The nature of multimedia*

In 1992 The Arts Council of Great Britain published a report entitled *Very Spaghetti: the potential of interactive multimedia in art galleries.*[9] In this report Richard Francis attempts to pin down the somewhat slippery nature of multimedia. He suggests,

> interactive multimedia has become the focus of increasing attention in the computer industry and is regarded by many as the next step for consumer product development. (The suggestion commonly voiced is that we will all be watching 'smart televisions' in the next century delivering developed interactive technology with multiple choice television channels). Open learning, home entertainment and market manipulations of our purchasing and opinion forming habits will be shipped to us in our living rooms (as they are quaintly defined) through the smartest box we have yet conceived.

He contrasts this with existing technology as follows:

> The significant differences between this technology and others is its ability to mimic an interaction with the user. You are able to ask questions of the machine and to be presented with responses and ideas which are the results of your interrogations without feeling controlled by the programme.

If we accept this definition, the sort of interaction which is promised by the new digital media will not be anything like the kind of social interaction that our great-grandparents remember. It will be an electronically-mimicked interaction.

The problem with accepting this definition, though, is that we have no way of knowing whether it will prove to be correct or not. Multimedia is at approximately the same stage of development that the cinema was when Mary Pickford was a star. It exists at the moment, here and there, in a variety of primitive forms, but the talk – the hype – is all about what it might be if, and when, it comes together. Asking Richard Francis (or anybody else for that matter) to define the ways in which multimedia might develop is a lot like asking Mack Sennett to define cinema in 1911 – and then berating him for not explaining how the special effects in *Star Wars* would be done.

There is not even an agreed language for discussing the processes and products of the nascent multimedia industry. The motion picture industry produces films; the record industry produces songs. The software industry produces programs or applications, which create things called files. Units of multimedia, however, are just – things. They have no particular shape or size or form. They are whatever they are, they last as long as they last, and they do whatever they do. They sit on floppy disks or CD-Roms; they are displayed in interactive booths at galleries, museums or shows; or they are distributed over the Internet.

If it is not advisable to attempt a definition of multimedia, it is nonetheless possible to describe the features that most of the current examples of multimedia seem to have in common.

Firstly, a multimedia piece is a **combination of different forms** of work, produced in different media or by using different computer programs. These might include photographs, paintings, text, moving images and sound. Of course, not everything that is claimed as multimedia work will necessarily contain all of these. A multimedia piece might be projected and amplified; it might be shown on televisions and monitors; or it might be displayed on specially modified headsets.

Secondly, a multimedia piece will usually be **interactive** within certain limits. This means that it will contain mechanisms that give the user the impression of controlling the action or the flow of information. These could be something as simple as buttons on a computer screen that say things like 'click here for more details' or 'click here to see the next exhibit'. They could be as complex as having a computer remember every action the user makes, and then having it adjust the range of options presented at each stage of the piece on the basis of the user's previous behaviour.

Thirdly, a multimedia piece will usually be designed to be **non-linear**. This means that the user will not be restricted to viewing the piece from the beginning to the end, but instead will be able to choose from a number of routes through the material. Indeed, there may not be a single end-point in a multimedia piece at all, and the routes through the material may be almost infinite.

Any number of computer-based adventure games could be used to provide an example of non-linearity. At a certain point in a game a player might see a row of six houses on the screen. Clicking on any of the six front doors might lead to a screen showing the view inside that particular house. Clicking on various parts of that screen might lead him or her into different rooms. In the front room, clicking on the television might switch it on, while clicking on a newspaper might show a close-up of the front page.

In this hypothetical example the first screen would lead into any of six possible second screens. Each one of these would lead into a large number of possible third screens, which would in turn lead to other screens containing more detailed information. If this were done properly then players could be given the illusion of wandering at will around an environment, rather than working their way through a predetermined narrative.

This kind of indeterminacy does not need to be moderated by a computer, however, and indeed it has been successfully published in book form. Over the last fifteen years Penguin have published at least fifty 'Fighting Fantasy' gamebooks (mostly written by Steve Jackson and Ian Livingstone) which have sold well to children and teenagers. These books consist of short numbered sections, and are played with a dice and a pencil. The reader begins by rolling the dice to establish the attributes of a character or group of characters. In Steve Jackson's book *Starship Traveller*, for example, the reader establishes a crew of seven, each of whom have 'skill' and 'stamina' ratings.

The short numbered sections of the book are not in narrative order. Section 1 finishes: 'an almighty explosion rocks the ship and all the crew, including you, lose consciousness. Turn to 256.'[10] This section then details the process of waking up again, and regaining control of the warp drive. You can see three solar systems ahead, two of which may bear life. It finishes by offering three choices. 'Will you press on towards the life-bearing system ahead (turn to 86); turn to port towards the other life-bearing system (turn to 273); or turn to starboard towards the barren system (turn to 142)?'[11] There are several different endings to the book, although there is only one 'successful' one.

The main problems with presenting interactivity in this format, however, are that it permits cheating through retracing one's steps, and it reveals, through the size of the book, approximately how many options there actually are. Both of these problems can be solved when entertainment like this is placed on a floppy disk or CD-Rom, and moderated by a computer. A computer program can ensure that it is impossible to cheat through backtracking, and the size of the files will not provide sufficient clues to gauge the overall size of the game. Placing the work on a computer would also make it possible to use moving images, speech, sound effects and music in addition to (or instead of) the text.

Creating this kind of entertainment for commercial distribution entails both narrative and programming skills. These programming skills themselves depend upon the existence of an internationally agreed set of standards and protocols for storing and recalling text, images and sounds on different computers.

4 *Computers and protocol*

In 1908 the first edition of the English-Esperanto Dictionary was published. In the introduction the compiler Joseph Rhodes wrote,

> it is now twenty-one years since the first English version of Dr. Zamenhof's little pamphlet appeared in print and Esperanto, which, in 1887, was a promising but untried system, has now taken its place ... as a practical auxiliary language, offering its services as a neutral yet efficient means of communication between all civilized nations.

He argued that there 'is now, however, no part of the globe reached by Western civilization to which the mails do not carry letters in the Auxiliary International Language', and from this he concluded that the progress of Esperanto was almost unstoppable – that it had 'refuted forever the prophecies of the incredulous and prejudiced'.

The advocates of Esperanto had conceived a brilliantly simple idea. If every schoolchild in every country was taught the same 'auxiliary language' then everybody would soon be able to communicate with everybody else. A Norwegian could make herself understood clearly in Frankfurt without knowing a word of German, while a Spaniard could conduct detailed business discussions in Stockholm. In the event, though, very few schoolchildren were ever actually taught Esperanto, and because very few people spoke the 'auxiliary international language' there was little incentive for any adult to learn it. Thus the project gradually dwindled, until today Esperanto is used only by small groups of hobbyists and devotees.

The current state of the digital revolution (the information superhighway, the wired world, the infobahn, or whatever it is being called this week) is in many ways similar to the position of Esperanto in 1908. To succeed, advocates of the superhighway need to persuade a very large number of people to sign up. More importantly, they need to provide all those who do sign up with the means to enable their computers to send and receive signals from each other. The digital revolution will depend on the availability of cheap but increasingly powerful computers; but it will also depend on these computers understanding the same 'language'.

This is not an entirely new problem. Computers have no inherent understanding of anything at all; they merely respond to whatever input they have been programmed to recognise. For a computer to communicate with anything other than itself it must have been programmed to do so. Computer users will probably be familiar with the varying degrees of frustration that can be involved in getting a computer to acknowledge the existence of a new printer, and then to print correctly using it.

Installing a printer almost always involves considerably more than simply plugging it into the computer and switching it on. The computer's operating system will not necessarily be able to communicate with the printer. Indeed the printer may be a new model, designed and manufactured after the computer was purchased. The user will almost certainly have to insert a floppy disk and copy a number of small programs into the operating system to enable the computer to send signals to, and receive messages from, the printer. The computer will then probably need to be switched off and restarted. Finally, individual word-processing programs might need to have their settings altered to enable them to format their pages to the correct size.

This process is necessary simply to enable a single computer to work in harmony with a specific printer. It would probably need to be repeated if the computer were to be used with a different printer. As a means of turning the world digital it is almost quaintly clumsy, and computer manufacturers, software engineers and others have invested considerable time in developing protocols which will generalise this and similar processes.

The earliest example of such a protocol was the introduction of ASCII in 1964 by the American Standards Association. This was designed to standardise the way in which computers received information from keyboards. Computers do not understand letters, numbers and punctuation, they only respond to binary numbers transmitted in the form of short pulses which are either on or off. In principle, then, a computer is no more able to understand input from a keyboard than it is able to understand messages sent by a printer.

When keyboards began to replace punched cards as the means of entering data into a computer, all computer manufacturers faced the same problem:

how to make the computer interpret the keystrokes correctly. Each manufacturer could have tackled the problem separately; however, this would not only have meant a duplication of effort, but would have guaranteed that the data produced by one computer was unintelligible to all other computers. It would also have meant that each computer would have required a custom-made keyboard, greatly adding to its cost.

ASCII – the American Standard Code for Information Interchange – was a protocol designed to alleviate these problems.[12] It provided a standard format for the transmission of keyboard input, which all computer manufacturers and software companies began to use. ASCII allowed for 128 different characters, although this was later doubled to 256.

ASCII codes simply record the keystrokes used to enter data. They do not store information about aspects of formatting, such as underlining or italicising, nor do they store information about the typeface and type size in which text appears on-screen. ASCII codes are not capable of reproducing the sophisticated paragraph formatting, and style sheets, that programs like WordPerfect and Microsoft Word are capable of recognising. However, all personal computers use ASCII as the basis for interpreting commands from a keyboard. Almost all word processors can open and save ASCII files. They can all use the same auxiliary language.

It is the existence of this language, this agreed protocol, that enables computers to 'talk' to each other, to be used together. Without a protocol such as this the information that was generated by one computer would be gibberish to any other type of computer.

5 *Performance and MIDI*

'Making your own music' used to conjure up a picture of homely groups gathered round the piano, singing from tattered sheet music while Uncle Arthur played a more or less accomplished accompaniment. From a modern perspective, one of the most noticeable aspects of this scene was that the entire activity was acoustic. Nobody plugged their instruments in, and nobody switched anything on. This was the way that music had been played in every culture from prehistoric times.

Music was played acoustically until the early 1950s, when Les Paul invented the electric guitar and then began pioneering the development of multi-tracked sound recording. From that point on, more and more popular music began to be played on electric equipment – equipment that needed to be plugged in and switched on.

For fifteen years or so, until the late 1960s, electronic instruments were really electronic versions of existing acoustic instruments. However, during this period, musicians began to develop styles that could not be reproduced except on electric instruments. The most obvious example of this kind of development is the electric guitar solo that is such a feature of rock music. It simply could *not* be played properly on an acoustic guitar, although an acoustic guitar could duplicate all the notes in the same order and with the same intervals. The *style* of an electric guitar solo, however, is not just built from the notes, the intervals between them, and the inflections with which they are played. It is also dependent on the particular sounds, the particular *timbres*, that become possible when music is played with amplified string instruments capable of having their sound distorted.

The development of electric instruments, and electric amplification, led musicians to experiment with timbres, with different kinds of sound and noise, as well as with different musical styles. This in turn led other people to become interested in the idea of producing completely new, hitherto unheard, timbres. In the late 1960s, as a result of an interest in these developments, Robert Moog produced an envelope generator, which modified sounds, and which formed the basis of the first Moog synthesiser.

Synthesisers are unlike any other musical instruments in that they do not have a 'natural voice'. A flute sounds like a flute, a bassoon sounds like a bassoon, and a cello sounds like a cello. Although you can play any of those instruments so that they don't sound with their natural voice, this would be a deliberately perverse action. Most people would think of a broadly similar kind of sound if they were asked to imagine the sound of a flute.

It would be ridiculous, though, to ask someone to think of the sound that a synthesiser makes, since synthesisers are designed to reproduce an almost infinite range of sounds. They do this by electronically processing one or more simple sine waves, and then altering them into various complex sound waves, according to the way they are programmed.

The original synthesisers produced by Robert Moog processed sound through valves and oscillators. These were temperamental, and liable to slide out of tune in cold weather, in hot weather, or even in a smoky room; so almost as soon as the idea of synthesising sounds had been conceived people began work on ways of producing the same effects more reliably. Within less than a decade this sound processing was being done by microprocessors and silicon chips; and today, if you open the top of a synthesiser, all you will find in there is a few circuit boards and chips. Today synthesisers are a specialised form of computer.

Although most manufacturers do their best to make the outside of a synthesiser look like a traditional keyboard, using it as near as possible like using any other musical instrument, and programming it a series of musical, rather than technical, decisions, the fact is that it is a computer. Inside it, as in any other computer, information is being received, stored and transmitted in binary code.

Synthesisers were not the only form of computerised musical instruments being developed during the 1970s, however. There were also drum machines which enabled musicians to programme a rhythm and have it played back using more or less realistic drum sounds. It was not long before people began to try to make these things work together, that is to synchronise them. There were a number of attempts at this, but each of them worked differently and with differing degrees of success. In 1983, after several years of work in Japan and at Sequential Circuits in California, an international standard for synchronising electronic instruments was agreed by all the major musical instrument manufacturers. This was MIDI – the musical instrument digital interface.

The manufacturers agreed that from 1983 all their electronic instruments would conform to the MIDI specifications. At its simplest MIDI is a method of linking two or more musical instruments together, so that they can play the same notes simultaneously or in harmony with each other. It is a way of playing one keyboard and having the notes sound like a flute and a pipe organ at the same time. However MIDI can be used to do much more than that. It can provide a way of controlling one or more synthesisers from a home computer, so that all the various parts of a piece of music that have been written into a computer program can be played back simultaneously through a range of electronic instruments.

The MIDI specifications start by giving every note a number, and they allow for 128 notes, having middle C as note 60. The data for each note in a piece of music has three basic components: the note number, information about the time the player began playing it (or the note was switched on), and information about the time the player released the note (or the note was switched off). The 'note on' and 'note off' information is usually stored as bars, beats and clicks (clicks being a 1/24 of a beat).

If a MIDI instrument is given a series of instructions from a computer in terms of note numbers with related note on and note off commands, it will play a sequence of notes as requested. However they will sound very mechanical because each note will be played with exactly the same pressure, and with no inflections at all. A set of secondary MIDI signals are available to deal with musical subtleties such as volume, pitch-bending and pedal-release. Used properly, these can enable a piece of music played via a computer to sound 'human'.

The instructions that the computer sends to the instrument can have been loaded into the computer in one of two ways. Firstly, they can be played into a computer program by a musician playing a keyboard which has its MIDI-out socket connected to a MIDI-in socket on the computer. Secondly, they can be typed directly into a computer program as a list of numbers, or drawn onto an on-screen set of staves. Of course, a mixture of the two processes is also possible, and this is what most musicians actually do: recording in real-time, by playing a keyboard and recording its MIDI signals onto a computer; and then editing it later in step-time – altering a wrong note, perhaps, or correcting an unintended inflection.

In addition to the capabilities already described, the MIDI specifications allow for 16 'channels'. A string of notes can be assigned a channel number in the same way that a musician might record a string of notes onto one channel of a multi-track tape recorder. When the music is played back, each instrument can be set to receive data on a different channel, so that each instrument can play a separate, but related, string of notes simultaneously. For example, one plays the bass, while the second plays the strings. One person, by recording instruments one after another onto different MIDI channels, can turn herself into an orchestra, a jazz band, or a rock group.

Because MIDI is a digital protocol its use is generalisable. It does not have to be used to produce music. The MIDI signals created on an electronic keyboard can be fed into an electronic lighting desk to produce a 'melodic' light show. Similarly MIDI signals can be generated by monitoring arrays of light beams placed across a space. Moving through a room can thus cause music to be played.

In doing any of this, people are using a carefully designed digital protocol to make several computers communicate with each other – even though they may never think of their synthesiser or lighting desk as a computer.

6 *Text and the Internet*

The beginnings of the Internet can be found in the establishment in 1969 of DARPANET, by the Defence Advanced Research Projects Agency, an offshoot of the US Defense Department. This was intended to enable researchers working at different universities, but engaged in militarily important projects, to exchange information.

When DARPANET was established the network consisted of just four large computers. By 1972 this had grown to 37 computers, and the name had changed to ARPANET. During the next 10 years the network continued to grow, and the ways in which it was used developed and mutated. The use of private electronic mailboxes began.

In 1983, the changing nature of the network was officially acknowledged when the Defense Department established a separate network, MILNET, to deal with sensitive or secret military research. In effect, this recognised the extent to which ARPANET was becoming a much more broadly-based phenomenon. At about the same time the National Science Foundation established a parallel network intended to connect educational establishments on a regional basis.

By 1990 these networks had grown beyond any of the founders' intentions. They had become the Internet. The number of users of the Internet has been estimated to be growing at the rate of 5 per cent per month. In December 1995, it was estimated that there are approximately 3,500,000 computers permanently attached to the Internet, and approximately 33,700,000 regular users.

For many people, the primary advantage of the Internet is its ability to connect users with computers all over the world for the price of a local phone call. They can send messages to people or organisations in other countries. They can receive electronic mail back from these people. They can also gain direct access to the information stored on many of these computers. This information can range from academic research papers, to databases of financial, legal and meteorological records, and to art in the form of text or images. Increasing numbers of people are publishing work directly onto the Internet, for others to read electronically.

To use the Internet, all that is necessary is access to a computer which is linked to the Internet. A university or a large company may have direct Internet access. This means, in effect, that they have a computer with dedicated telephone lines which are left switched on 24 hours a day, so that other users can reach them at any time of the day or night. Most small businesses, arts organisations and individuals, however, have an account with a service provider such as Demon, Easynet or Cityscape. They will then use their home computer and modem to log onto the computer of their service provider, in order to gain access to the Internet. While Internet access is theoretically free, service providers charge their users monthly fees. For most private users this fee is considerably less than the cost of maintaining and financing the computer and telephone lines which would be necessary to gain 'free' access. The fee also allows private users to leave the complex business of understanding the underlying technical aspects of the Internet's workings to their service provider.

When a user in London wants to send a message to somebody using a computer linked to the Internet in, say, Los Angeles, they will dial the local number of their Internet service provider (unless they are directly connected). From here they will gain access to the whole Internet. They will type their message, address it and then send it. Special router software will establish the most efficient route for sending the message from London to Los Angeles. It will be sent from the service provider's computer to the first computer on the chosen route; and from here to the second computer; and so on until it arrives at its destination. All the user has had to pay for is the original call to the service provider.

This process works because the Internet has grown as a federated system of computers, all of which constantly pass messages back and forth to their neighbours on the network. The Internet is probably unique in the way that it has grown and in the fact that nobody owns it or controls it. It works in the gaps left between the 'real work' of the computers that comprise it. There are committees that govern major aspects of the Net's management, but they have no absolute power. The Internet works only through co-operation and agreement upon mutually shared goals.

Among the fundamental agreements that enable the Internet to work are the software standards and protocols that ensure that all the computers attached to the Net are able to understand each other, and that information can be sent successfully across the network; and the addressing system that enables information to be transferred across the Net and reach the right destination.

The basic protocol used for transferring information is called IP – Internet Protocol. This divides all data sent across the Internet into packets, each of which is given its own address information. Each packet is sent separately by the router software, and the data is then reassembled into a single file when it reaches its destination. The advantage of this mechanism is that it makes the most efficient use of the gaps left between the 'real work' of the computers that comprise the Internet. Rather than trying to transfer very large files, it is simpler to transfer many more tiny files. The most commonly used version of this protocol is known as TCP/IP, which stands for Transmission Control Protocol/Internet Protocol. This is designed to enable different kinds of computer to transmit data to, and receive data from, each other.[13]

The Internet is not a single entity, with a single centralised telephone directory. It is, in fact, a loosely confederated network of networks. These range from academic networks to USENET, which is an area devoted to discussions on everything ranging from radical theology and Star Trek to embroidery and Third World campaigning.

The possibilities inherent in such a global network of networks have spurred on the development of ideas such as hypertext, as more and more people have realised that the Internet could be used for much, much more than transmitting e-mail and text files.

7 *Hypertext and the web*

1995 saw an explosion of popular interest in the Internet. Much of this interest was based on developments taking place in the fastest growing area of the Internet, the World Wide Web. The Web is based on a series of protocols which were first developed at the European Laboratory for Particle Physics (known as CERN) in Switzerland in 1990.

The fundamental protocol is HTML – hypertext mark-up language. This allows for the publication of fully graphical pages of hypertext: text which can be used as an on-screen 'button' that can be clicked on to provide an instant link to another page. These pages are beginning to contain not only text, but also full-colour images, sounds and movies.

It is important to realise that on the Web one page of a publication may be stored on a computer thousands of miles away from the 'next' page in what appears to be one document, although the user will still get the impression of browsing through a single document. Hypertext can provide links not just between different documents on a single computer, but between documents stored anywhere on the Internet.

The idea of hypertext[14] originated with Ted Nelson, who first began talking about it over 25 years ago. At that time his ideas seemed utopian at best, since not only were the concepts he was proposing unfamiliar but the computers that would be needed to make them work did not yet exist on anybody's drawing board.

In 1974 he self-published a book which was really two books in one – *Computer Lib* and *Dream Machines*. These were bound in such a way that each book started with a front cover and worked its way towards the middle of the combined volume.

In *Dream Machines* Nelson wrote,

> paper media, whatever their disadvantages, have at least been compatible; you could store the books, magazines and notes on the same shelf, compare them on the same desktop. Not for the new media, whether electronic or optical or magnetic or computerised. Each one

needs a separate device. You cannot presently make margin notes on a video tape. I say it will all have to come together again. We need a presentational and archival medium that can be as standard as paper, to reunify the present mess of separately beautiful and mutually unintelligible forms of storage, presentation and annotation. The hope may be a shared-standard data structure.[15]

The structure that he proposed was named Xanadu. He defined the Xanadu system as 'just one thing: a new form of interconnection for computer files – corresponding to the interconnection of ideas – which can be refined and elaborated into a shared network.' He added that 'if you truly understand this form of interconnection, you will understand its revolutionary potential.'[16]

The Xanadu project has never been completed, although work has progressed on it in one way or another for approximately thirty years. It has become one of the legends of the computer industry, both for its breadth of vision and for Ted Nelson's apparent inability ever to declare it finished. Even if Xanadu never actually appears it will have been of immense significance. Largely through the efforts of Ted Nelson, hypertext became a familiar term at computer conferences and shows, and a number of computer programs now exist which have successfully borrowed from some of the concepts that are central to Xanadu.

Of the hypertext-like programs currently available, HyperCard is perhaps the best known – not least because, for several years, it was given away free with every Apple Macintosh sold. HyperCard is best described as a programming toolbox that enables non-programmers to build their own mini-programs. The files HyperCard creates are known as 'stacks', and they consist of 'cards' of information, which can be written or pictorial, and can include sounds, animations and movies.

HyperCard works with a specially designed language called HyperTalk.[17] Instead of writing a single program which tells the computer everything it needs to know in order to do what you want it to do, you write lots of short instructions which you attach to 'objects'. Then, every time the user clicks the mouse while they are over an object, the computer will run the 'script' attached to that object. For example:

```
on mouseUp
     beep 2
     go next card
end mouseUp
```

This is a HyperTalk 'script', as these mini-programs are called, which could be attached to a button somewhere on the screen. If the user put their cursor over the button, then pressed and released their mouse button, the script would be activated. On 'mouseUp' (ie when the mouse button was released), the computer would beep twice and go to the next 'card', or screenful of information in the stack.

Imagine rewriting this book as a HyperCard stack. While it remains a book which is designed to be printed, stored and sold, there are a number of problems. Books have to be certain lengths, usually multiples of 4 or 16 pages. There will be money to print only a certain number of copies. If there are embarrassing factual errors I will be unable to correct them until (and only if) a second edition is printed. I will be able to include only a certain number of footnotes, because too many will crowd out the text, or make the book longer than the publisher is willing to print.

As a HyperCard stack these problems will disappear. It can be any length at all, up to the size that will fit on a floppy disk or CD-Rom. If it is made available on one or more floppy disks, the publisher will not need to print and store any copies in advance, since they can be duplicated to meet whatever demand there is – on a daily basis, if necessary. Factual errors can be corrected on the master disk as soon as they are pointed out, and outdated text can be replaced in the same way.

Most importantly, however, the problem of footnotes will disappear, because the links in HyperCard do not have to be linear. In the example above, the script could have said:

'go card forty'

The thirty-nine cards between the first and the fortieth could all have contained footnotes. These footnotes might be activated by clicking on perhaps words in italics on the main cards – words which would, in fact, be other buttons.

The effect of this would be that readers who, for example, wanted to know more about HyperTalk itself, could click on the italicised word to take them to another card, whereas those readers who already knew, or didn't want to know, could read on without having their flow of concentration interrupted. Moreover, this process of layering information can be as many layers deep as necessary. Footnotes can themselves lead to further footnotes, so that the user may follow an information trail like a fly crawling on a cat's cradle.

These features, among many others, make hypertext a breakthrough in dealing with complex information of many kinds. Stacks are already used by Ford in America to train mechanics, precisely because they can skim across all the stages of an operation they are comfortable with, but dive down as deeply as they need into the information pool in the stages where they are uncomfortable or where there are techniques with which they are unfamiliar.

Programs such as HyperCard[18] are designed to work on a single computer. The power of the World Wide Web is that the principle of non-linear links can be extended to cover information on any computer anywhere in the world that is attached to the Internet. A footnote in a book about witches might make reference to a scene in *Macbeth*. A website about witches might make a link to the same scene in *Macbeth* held on a computer at an American university. The difference, however, is that the electronic link would be a pointer to a specific part of the complete text of the play. The reader would be able to flip back to the piece about witches, or continue reading *Macbeth*, or follow up another link that was within the text of *Macbeth*.

This process of non-linear browsing is at the heart of the cultural importance of the digital revolution.

8 *The road to Nowhere*

Imagine, if you can, that you are overcome with a burning desire to make a large table-top model railway layout, complete with detailed 00-gauge scenery.

Perhaps you are a parent trying to interest your children in a traditional pastime for which they have little enthusiasm. Perhaps you are a hobbyist trying to recreate the minutiae of a busy railway station of the 1950s. Perhaps you are a sculptor concerned with producing a piece of social realism about public transport.

You might well begin by stretching chicken-wire into the approximate shape of an imaginary countryside – tugging it and pinching it until it is the shape that you require. Having fixed the wire to some hardboard, you might then cover it with papier mâché, perhaps adding some tiny stones to simulate gravel or rocks. Then you might paint it, carefully placing some model trees and buildings on the landscape, and perhaps positioning a small sliver of glass to simulate the reflective surface of a lake.

The landscape that you created could be viewed from any angle. You could take photographs of it – long shots of large parts of the countryside or close-ups of details. If you were accurate enough in your model-making, some of the photographs might fool people into thinking they were looking at a real landscape.

Using digital tools, you could follow a very similar procedure to construct an imaginary landscape that existed only inside a computer. This too could be 'photographed' from any angle in close-up or long shot, and some of these 'photographs' might fool people into thinking they were looking at a real landscape.

To produce an imaginary landscape inside a computer you would begin by using a modelling program. Metatool's KPT Bryce is such a program, designed for producing imaginary landscapes.[19] This program first creates 'wire-frame' images of terrains, equivalent to the chicken-wire frames of the model railway hobbyist. These can be stretched, twisted, and reshaped. Any number of them can be joined together to form a landscape. Flat planes can be dropped onto the landscape to serve as the surface of water. Objects can then be added to the landscape by manipulating basic core shapes, such as cones, cubes and circles, and then combining them.

Every surface can then be covered with a texture, which can be taken from the built-in selection, imported from a painting program, or created mathematically within Bryce. This process is known as rendering. The rendered landscape is not a picture – a computer-generated graphic. It is a fully fledged countryside that can be viewed from any angle and at any magnitude.

Using the on-screen controls, it is possible to zoom in on a scene or to move out; to move round objects to see their sides and rear; to view a scene from the sky, from head height, or from ground level. Any view can then be 'photographed' and the 'photograph' saved and printed out.

When a scene is 'photographed' a process called ray-tracing is utilised. This determines the position of the light source in an image and then works out how light would move through the image, allowing for reflective and transparent surfaces. It calculates shadows and reflections (and the reflections of shadows on some surfaces). From this it constructs an image that accurately represents the highlights, midtones and shadows in the imaginary scene.

In Bryce, this process involves positioning the sun, which means that you can 'photograph' the same scene from the same position at different times of day or night. It also involves determining the height, density and nature of the clouds, which can act as filters for the 'sunlight'. Finally, fog or mist can be added to further filter and distort the sunlight. Textures can be assigned degrees of transparency or reflectivity, which will determine how the computer-generated light reacts when it reaches their surface.

On an Apple Macintosh or a PC, a detailed image which is being rendered and ray-traced can take several hours to complete, as the program works out the intensely complex mathematical calculations needed to describe the movement of light over the surfaces, and the resultant light and dark. On most games consoles, however, a simplified version of this process happens in real time. On games such as *Super Mario Kart* or *Starfox* on the Super Nintendo,[20] for example, the environment within which the game takes place is a wireframe construction which can be viewed from any angle, and is constantly being texture mapped as the game proceeds.

The ability to create three-dimensional landscapes which can be texture mapped in real time and then viewed from any angle is at the heart of the development of virtual reality, a term first used by Jaron Lanier, the inventor of the dataglove, which was designed to enable a computer to interpret hand movements and respond to them. For Lanier 'virtual reality affects the outside world and not the inside world. Virtual reality creates a new objective level of reality.'[21]

One of the leading British companies in this field is W Industries, based in Leicester. They are a small company, employing about 70 people, although they have produced games booths for venues such as the Trocadero, as well as engaging in research projects with companies such as Sega and Paramount. They were founded in 1987 by Jon Waldern, and trade as Virtuality Entertainment. In 1993 their turnover was just under £6,000,000.

Virtuality designed and made the headsets which are now among the clichés of virtual reality. The headsets contain two tiny television-screens which are fed moving stereo images from a computer. These images are of the three-dimensional landscape through which the wearer is 'moving'. When worn, they enable the computer to track the movements of the wearer's head and adjust the images that are projected accordingly. If the wearer moves their head to the left, then they 'see' what is to the left of them in the virtual environment, and when they move their head to the right again their view of the 'landscape' changes accordingly. The headsets also contain speakers, so that the wearer can hear things approaching, and look around to see what direction they are approaching from.

The Virtuality system uses computer chips which have been specially designed to handle complex graphics. A recent magazine article claimed that hardware 'this fast enables you to create a full-colour 3D world which is able to move and follow your movements at about 10 frames per second. This doesn't sound a lot but it's enough to give you the ride of your life'.[22] Frankly, this is an enthusiastic overstatement since at present this kind of virtual reality cannot quite keep up with sudden movements of the human head. If the user moves their head rapidly from side to side, then the images they see will lag noticeably behind, and they will probably lose their bearings. Nonetheless the kind of immersive pseudo-reality that these systems offer can go a long way towards placing the user 'inside' the geography of the model railway layout, and can offer an interesting opportunity to walk down the streets of an imaginary town.

Silicon Graphics is a company that has been at the forefront of 3D computer graphics for over a decade. In 1984 they introduced the first SGI workstation, which cost $80,000. In 1993 they sold over $1 billion of graphics workstations. Since 1990 their founder, Jim Clark, has been convinced that 'the future lies in things like cable-TV boxes and digital game players'.[23] They have developed and recently demonstrated a programming language called VRML – virtual reality mark-up language.

VRML is designed to bring virtual reality to the on-line world of the World Wide Web. With the aid of a small 'helper program' it will enable people to access the World Wide Web and meet other people there in simulated 3D environments. People will be able to walk around these environments, meeting other people as they go.

Other companies are working in parallel areas towards similar ends. The American company Worlds Inc.[24] has launched a prototype Internet site called AlphaWorld:

> This is a kind of 3D virtual metropolis in progress… Originally the company invited around 400 people to take up residence there. However, thousands of would-be virtual homesteaders have since crashed the virtual party and created hundreds of digital buildings – virtual galleries, suburbs, bars. They've even begun to put out a newspaper, the *New World Times*.'[25]

The aim of all of these experiments is to create worlds that have no real existence outside a computer: worlds that exist nowhere in the real world. These worlds, however, will be consistent, and they will be completely navigable. With the right equipment they will be 'real': that is, the user will become so immersed in them that he or she will treat them as though they were real.

The road to Nowhere will not, by definition, be discovered, since it does not exist in what we call the real world. It will be created by deliberate design, that is, by people using digital tools which operate through digital protocols. What we will find when we get to Nowhere will be entirely up to the people who are creating it. They will decide whether it has gravity, or whether it has levity.

Some of these people are working, or have worked, in the traditional arts. Some are enthusiasts, hobbyists or obsessives. Some are working for large corporations whose vision of the future is altogether more commercial. There is a necessary tentativeness to all the current work, and it is by no means certain whether the digital revolution will place the work of artists at the centre of the electronic stage, or at its periphery.

One thing is certain, however. Nobody will stand any chance at all of acting on the silicon stage unless they decide to start making footprints in the sand.

Footprints in the sand

'Art is meant to disturb, science reassures.'

Georges Braque

9 *Prefabricated melody*

Music, as Frank Zappa once noted, is simply 'decorated time'.

Zappa has written that 'a person with a feel for rhythm can walk into a factory and hear the machine noise as a composition.'

> If something can be conceived as music, it can be executed as music, and presented to an audience in such a way they will perceive it as music... Music in performance is a type of sculpture... Things which make sounds are things which are capable of creating perturbations. These perturbations modify (or sculpt) the raw material (the 'static air' in the room – the way it was 'at rest' before the musicians started fucking around with it). If you purposefully generate atmospheric perturbations ('air shapes') then you are composing.[26]

Music, then, consists of a series of sounds or 'perturbations' that are played in a specific sequence. Conventionally, these 'sounds' are series of notes of specific pitches played on musical instruments which produce these pitches with predictable timbres. This does not have to be the case though, and there are many composers, apart from members of the avant-garde, who have used 'non-musical' sounds within compositions. Tchaikovsky's *1812 Overture* provides one example of a popular 'conventional' piece of music which includes 'non-musical' noises (in this case cannon) as an integral part of its score.

The obvious attraction for composers and performers of conventional musical instruments over other 'non-musical' sound sources is the predictability of instruments – and especially their predictable ability to play sounds of a similar timbre at different pitches. However, digital samplers now give musicians the ability to use any sound as the basis of a predictable musical palette. Samplers will play an arpeggio of cash registers, or a minor chord of bottles breaking, or a thud pitched at the G below middle C – and they will play it the same way every time.

Composers have made use of samplers for many reasons. Some have come to believe that orchestral musicians were either unable or unwilling to learn their pieces sufficiently well to perform them accurately, and have been moved to create them themselves, part by part. Others have used sampling for altogether different purposes.

In 1987 Bill Drummond and Jimmy Cauty made a single called *All You Need Is Love*, under the name The Justified Ancients of MuMu.[27] The single was 'a coarse, hard-hitting attack at the media coverage of the AIDS crisis, featuring samples of BBC broadcasts, the Beatles, and Samantha Fox. It was released on the JAMs own label – The Sound of Mu (sic).'[28] They followed this with an album – *1987: what the fuck's going on?* – which was constructed almost entirely from samples, drum machines and vocals. The samples were used iconoclastically. They made points, they underlined arguments, or they provided an ironic comment on the song in which they were included. Sometimes this song itself provided an ironic comment on the original pieces that were used in it as samples.

Shortly after its release, in a letter to Bill Drummond, the Mechanical Copyright Protection Society Ltd (MCPS), wrote,

> since you did not comply with the provisions of Section 8 of the 1956 Copyright Act and 1957 Copyright Royalty System (Records) Regulations in the submission of Statutory Notices, not less than 15 days prior to the release of the records, or paid royalties within the stipulated time period in respect of the works controlled by our members, the records so far manufactured have infringed copyright.
>
> Furthermore, our solicitors have advised us that even if you had abided by the above, the very nature of making a record of a work which comprises a part of a work takes this outside of Section 8 and would, therefore, require the prior permission of the copyright holders. Certain works which you have used have also been clearly arranged, which may not be done without the consent of the owners of these works.
>
> One of our members, whose work is used substantially on the *1987* album is not prepared to grant a licence in respect of their work.

The last sentence refers to the track *The Queen & I*, which used a sample of almost all of Abba's *Dancing Queen*. The MCPS, on behalf of Abba, successfully demanded that the record be withdrawn; that the JAMs 'take all possible steps to recover copies of the album which are then to be delivered to MCPS or destroyed under the supervision of MCPS'; and that the master tapes be surrendered to the MCPS.

Bill Drummond's response was,

> if machines were going to be invented like samplers, you can't stop
> them. Its like inventing the electric guitar and saying – well you can't
> play them. It seemed just like all the acoustic guitarists saying – afraid
> that's it boys, you can't play the electric guitar.[29]

He argued that in a media-saturated world composers had a right to treat
media output as the raw material with which they worked.

When, in the eighteenth century, people walked through the countryside
or through the streets of a town their environment was by and large silent
except for the sounds of animals, and of people talking, singing and
whistling. It was from this environment that artists drew their inspiration.
Today people are everywhere brought into contact with pre-programmed
messages: advertisements, posters, neon signs, logos on t-shirts, elevator
music, in-store radio stations, and other people's Walkmans. This is the
environment within which work is created today.

Traditionally, classical composers 'borrowed' folk tunes, or included
references to other compositions in their work. They did this because the
material that was being quoted or reworked provided cultural reference
points for the music. In the late twentieth century a snippet of Nelson
Mandela speaking, the theme tune to *The X-Files*, a pirate radio jingle, or
the piano motif in Moby's *Hymn*, might conceivably provide a similar
cultural reference point.

The JAMs were able to create their work only because the technology
existed to enable them to do so. They had a moral and aesthetic argument
to justify their activities, but inevitably this argument meant nothing in
the face of the economic imperatives of international copyright law. From
then on the JAMs were forced to seek permission to use samples.[30]

John Oswald is a Canadian who has used the techniques of sampling in an
even more extreme way than the JAMs. He produced a compact disc
entitled *Plunderphonics*, which he distributed privately and without
charging any fee. Even though it was clearly marked NOT FOR SALE,
Michael Jackson, Sony Records and the Canadian Recording Industry
Association all declared his work illegal, and forced him to cease
distributing it.

The term 'plunderphonics' came from a paper that Oswald delivered to
the 1985 Wired Society Electro-Acoustic conference in Toronto entitled
'Plunderphonics, or audio piracy as a compositional prerogative'.[31] In this,

Oswald advanced a sophisticated set of arguments which broadly paralleled Bill Drummond's opinions. In a processed world it is necessarily permissible, and probably inevitable, to take work that other people have cooked up and use it as raw material for your own creativity.

The *Plunderphonics* EP contains liner notes by English musician and author David Toop, in which he notes that, when you buy a piece of recorded music, you have 'the privilege of ignoring the artist's intentions. You can take two copies of the same record, run through them with an electric drill, warp them on the stove, fill the grooves with fine sand and play them off-centre and out of phase at half speed.' The ownership of sound is more complex, then, than the legal mechanisms that currently protect 'intellectual property'.[32]

As a result of the reception of the *Plunderphonics* EP, John Oswald was commissioned to produce a piece of work for the Kronos Quartet for their album *Short Stories*. Oswald spent a day with the quartet:

> I got Kronos to do very simple things – play open strings, glisses, transitions between notes, certain shapes over a period of time. We recorded for about ten hours, with the whole group and individuals. Some things they played together, some solo.[33]

From these samples of the Kronos Quartet in action, Oswald composed a piece *Spectre* on a digital editing suite.

At the request of Phil Lesh,[34] he has recently worked with the Grateful Dead to produce a double CD called *Grayfolded*. For this he worked with tapes of the Grateful Dead's live performances. Specifically, he listened to several hundred versions of *Dark Star*, the song that the Grateful Dead used as the basis for lengthy and varied improvisations. From these tapes he has produced two extraordinary sixty-minute pieces, *Transitive Axis* and *Mirror Ashes*, in which, among other things, the vocalists from one decade harmonise with their younger selves, and the young Jerry Garcia duets with his middle-aged self. Whole performances are speeded up and folded in on themselves to provide percussive sounds.

Not all sampling has been as blatant, and as deliberately controversial, as the KLF's recordings or John Oswald's plunderphonics. Much sampling has been intended to do nothing more than build a musical collage over which more instruments and vocals can be added. This kind of sampling has become a core element of rap music, and a staple part of much other dance music. Today, however, it is almost always undertaken only after permission has been obtained from the creator of the work being sampled, and a fee agreed for its use.

Even where the intention of the sampling is more adventurous, permission is usually sought. The release of the Orb's single *Little Fluffy Clouds*, for example, was delayed until Rickie Lee Jones agreed that part of a radio interview with her could be used as a vocal refrain.

The reaction of copyright holders to requests to sample their work in this way has varied considerably. Some people have attempted to maintain complete control of their work, while others have cheerfully relinquished it. George Clinton,[35] whose work has been endlessly sampled for rap and hiphop records, has gone as far as to produce two compact discs of material specifically designed for sampling. For the two volumes of *Sample Disc, Sample DAT* Clinton took the master tapes of his most influential work back into a studio, and used them to produce approximately two hundred short extracts which could be used straight from the compact disc. Each is completely functional, consisting of a set number of bars of a riff or motif. The discs come with a slip to apply to use the samples, and a sliding scale of payments.[36]

One of the few people in recent years to use samples as a major part of their work, without seeking permission for their inclusion, has been the London-based Scanner. His work begins with the use of scanning equipment to intercept private digital telephone conversations which he records and collages. 'Once a week I switch the scanner on, connect it straight to the tape deck and just record everything I flick through. I build up a library of sounds of conversations.'[37] Taking care to remove anything that might identify the individual voices, he uses the scans as the basis of ambient musical pieces for live performance at raves and 'art events', and for release on compact disc. In May 1995 he created a three-week radio show for the Videopositive Festival in Liverpool, mixing together sounds scanned and recorded in the city. Since then he has recorded his third compact disc, *Sulphur*, at a live event at the Purcell Rooms in London.

Scanner is part of a growing group of British musicians working in what might be termed popular digital music. These range from Spooky, whose work spans DJ-ing and writing for *Artforum*, and Tricky and his collaborative project Nearly God in Bristol, to the Brighton-based Dave Clarke whose three singles *Red*, and new album *Archive One*, were heralded by reviewers as the beginning of 'intelligent techno'. They also include the sound and performance work of groups like Hex, whose Matt Black was half of the seminal Eighties' sampling duo Coldcut.

All of these are clearly determined to continue to find new ways of decorating time with a mixture of new and prefabricated materials.

10 *Musically alive environments*

Creative movements tend to begin in one of two ways. Either they develop organically out of existing work, and are identified and labelled retrospectively; or they are deliberately created – arriving fully fledged, with a manifesto, a name and accompanying terminology.

The birth of rock and roll provides a musical example of organic development. It was born out of a combination of the blues and country music. There is no real agreement about who 'invented' rock and roll, or what the first rock and roll record was, although it is generally accepted that the disc jockey Alan Freed was the first person to use the actual term 'rock and roll'.

Ambient music, on the other hand, is an example of a musical genre which arrived fully fledged. It was 'invented' by Brian Eno in 1972.

Brian Eno had produced music which was directly concerned with ideas of indeterminacy and multilinearity. He had produced and sold *Oblique Strategies*, a pack of playing cards each of which contained a single instruction, such as 'Go slowly all the way round the outside', 'Don't be afraid of things because they are easy to do', 'Only a part and not the whole', or 'Is it finished?'. The idea of these was that artists would use the pack to get out of creative logjams by shuffling it, taking a card and then trying to obey the instruction within the context of the piece being constructed.

Later Eno became the producer of U2's most successful records; a collaborator with David Bowie, Laurie Anderson, Peter Gabriel and many others; and Visiting Professor of Fine Arts at the Royal College of Art.

The ideas behind ambient music arose when Eno was lying in bed ill, listening to some quiet music. One of the speakers on his record player ceased functioning, and he found himself listening to half the intended musical information at a fraction of the intended volume. He became intrigued by the possibility of deliberately creating music to operate in these conditions: to be played at such a quiet volume that it ceased to hold the attention and became part of the overall ambience of the environment.

The first recording that Eno created with these principles in mind was *Discreet Music*[38] the notes of which include a full description of the reasons behind the music and a diagram explaining the techniques used to produce it.

> The system used two tape recorders set up so that when a single sound was played, it was heard several seconds later at a slightly lower volume level, then again several seconds later at a still lower volume level, and so on … New sounds could thus be introduced and layered on top of the old ones without erasing them. The repeated looped signal – typically about five seconds long – could be allowed to repeat and decay indefinitely.[39]

Eno used this technique in his collaborative work with the musician Robert Fripp, who himself used it for a series of solo recordings and live performances,[40] as well as incorporating the technique into much of his other work.

Eno's early development of ambient music took place in the 1970s, before personal computers and well before the advent of the MIDI protocol. It was all undertaken using analogue equipment. Both Brian Eno and Robert Fripp have continued to do this kind of work. However, they have both switched to digital equipment because, Fripp says, 'the profusion and development of [electronic] effects units, and the advent of MIDI control during the past decade have made possible a proliferation of choice and opportunities in the moment of shaping sound.'[41]

Robert Fripp describes his recent work in this vein as 'improvised and largely governed by the time, place, audience and the performer's response to them'; adding,

> if the reader protests that it is obvious and self-evident that this must be so, that performances unfold in the time of their unfolding, I can only reply that most musical situations of my experience pay little attention to the time, place and personae of the musical event.[42]

Robert Fripp now refers to this area of his work as soundscaping. A comparative listening to *Let The Power Fall*, which was recorded in 1981 using analogue machinery to manipulate the sounds of the guitar, and *1999*, which was released in 1995 using digital equipment to shape the sounds, provides an interesting insight into the very practical differences that the use of digital equipment can make. Both recordings were made with the same objectives: to improvise pieces based on looping sounds which responded directly to the place in which they were being played and the people in attendance. The palette of sounds that Fripp can draw upon, and the subtlety with which they can be manipulated, is unquestionably larger and more varied in the digital recordings.

The term 'ambient music' has recently become popularised both in phrases such as 'ambient dub', and as a general term to describe music that is quiet and repetitive. The work of a disparate group of people ranging from Moby, The Orb and Jah Wobble to Terry Riley, Michael Nyman and the Penguin Café Orchestra has from time to time been characterised as 'ambient'.

The term was originally intended to describe a music which did not impose itself on the listener but remained in the background as part of the overall environment. The use of endlessly repeating patterns of musical motifs was simply a means to this end. The distinguishing feature of the music was not intended to be the use of repetition. Repetition was merely a strategy to prevent the music from becoming too interesting in a conventional sense. If it were to become too interesting it would inevitably begin to draw attention to itself, and thus cease to be part of the background ambience.[43] The real distinguishing feature of ambient music was it was created to be perceived as an integral part of an architectural space.[44]

The relationship between music and space is something that has concerned David Jackson for some years. Since 1990 one of David Jackson's recurring activities has been to tour his one-man performance *Tonewall* within Britain and the rest of Europe. He describes this as featuring 'saxophones, flutes, whistles, panpipes and percussion; played in conjunction with a wall of studio equipment which provides the accompaniment and magical special effects'.[45]

At the heart of the wall of studio equipment is an electronic system called Soundbeam.[46] This is 'a system using ultrasonic pulses to detect movements and turn these into instructions for controlling electronic musical instruments'[47]. The system works on a similar principle to the sonar that is used in submarines for measuring depth. It consists of a number of transceivers, which can both send and receive ultrasonic pulses up to a distance of seven metres. The pulses operate as a cone: that is, the further a pulse is from the transceiver that sent it the wider the beam.

Each beam can be assigned up to seven different responses which are triggered by interrupting the beam, and causing it to be deflected back to the transceiver. If the beam were set to respond to its maximum seven-metre length, then an interruption anywhere in the first metre of the beam would cause response A; an interruption somewhere between one and two metres would trigger response B; and so on.

The responses are MIDI signals, which can be used to trigger any MIDI event in any MIDI device. Using a sequencer and synthesiser, each signal can be used to trigger a single noise, a drum or percussion sound, a musical note, a chord, a scale or an arpeggio.

The result of this is that when a number of beams are set up so that they cover a large part of an enclosed space, the space itself becomes musically alive. Moving through the space will cause music to be produced. The kind of music that happens, and the degree to which it is harmonious or discordant, will depend on the sounds and MIDI events that have been programmed into the sequencers and synthesisers triggered by each beam.

David Jackson has used this to collaborate with other artists in exploring dance, mime and storytelling and their relationship to group music-making. He is also firmly convinced of the value of this as a tool for working with 'people with restricted movement. Whatever their disability, this system allows people to make music together as equals.'[48] The range of music that people can make is not limited by their possible range of movement. The beams can be repositioned, and their depth of response adjusted, until their settings are the most suitable for the participants. Each beam can be set to respond to a minimum distance of 25 centimetres – which means that the difference between triggering response A and response B can be a movement of just over three centimetres.

The creation of such musically active spaces is not necessarily an indoor activity. At Bracknell Park in Berkshire, Jackson has produced outdoor sound sculptures by setting the beams to respond with long slow drones to leaves falling from the trees. This process created a kind of circular ambient music in which it was the behaviour of the environment itself that created the sounds, which thus formed, from the outset, a 'natural' part of that environment.

11 *The composer dances*

David Jackson's use of the *Tonewall* is at its most traditionally 'artistic' when he performs one-man concerts. He creates a varied but always interesting music which is mostly, but not entirely, improvised. He does this by using a combination of traditionally played wind instruments, electronic effects pedals, and a constant interaction with a number of soundbeams.

Viewed from the audience, Jackson can seem to be playing the saxophone in an extraordinarily odd and mannered way – ducking and diving, bobbing and weaving, while all the time making strange jerky movements with his elbows and upper body. Many people have taken this movement to be nothing more than a personal idiosyncrasy, because they have assumed that, in a conventional way, he is playing a solo over backing music which has either been previously taped or is being generated automatically by pre-programmed sequencers.

In reality, however, David Jackson is dancing all the sounds into existence, except those of the saxophone (or flute, or whatever he has in his mouth at that moment). The rhythm parts and the orchestral accompaniment exist only because his physical movements are interrupting the soundbeam in a way that has become predictable to him through years of practice. Individual elements are, of course, pre-programmed and loaded into sequencers. The synthesiser voices – the actual noises that each synthesiser makes when it plays middle C or any other note – have also been carefully selected and refined over a long period, and are programmed in before the performance.

With the exception (sometimes) of a simple underlying drone, pulse or rhythm which is switched on at the start of a piece, and which remains constant throughout it, all the synthesisers and sequencers on-stage will remain silent unless they receive a signal from one or other of the beams. The beams will only send signals when they are interrupted by a movement.

Even when he appears to be using a traditional format, with the performer on the stage and the audience seated in front of him, Jackson is still working within a physical space which has been rendered musically active. In order to perform his music, David Jackson *has* to dance.

Jackson is by no means alone in exploring this area. The idea of creating musically active spaces, and then dancing music into existence, is one that Rolf Gehlhaar, for example, has been pursuing since at least 1985.

Rolf Gehlhaar is an internationally recognised composer, living and working in north London. He spent four years as Karlheinz Stockhausen's personal assistant, as well as participating in at least twelve of his recordings. He has spent time researching at IRCAM in Paris, and CERM in Metz, as well as the Electronic Studio of West German Radio in Cologne. Thus his interest in the possibilities of electronic music predates the advent of digital equipment. He wrote many pieces in the 1970s which explored the possibilities of tape delay. His piece *Solipse*, for example, was written in 1973 for solo cello and tape delay; while *Polymorph* was written in 1978 for bass clarinet and tape delay.

In 1985 he 'designed the first version of "Sound-Space", a computer-controlled interactive musical environment in which the public creates, influences and can play with the music it hears, merely by moving about in a space. As a result of a commission by the Museum of Science and Industry at la Villette in Paris, this first version was permanently installed there in 1986.'[49]

Gehlhaar's background and interests are such that he designed and built the first version of 'Sound-Space' entirely by himself. The original software was written in the computer language Basic on an Apple Macintosh, and was designed as 'composing software that would respond in an interesting way to input it received'.[50] Subsequently, like many musicians, he began working on an Atari ST – and still does.

Superficially, Gehlhaar's 'Sound-Space' can seem very similar to the Soundbeam that David Jackson uses in his *Tonewall* performances. Gehlhaar himself has described 'Sound-Space' as 'the real-time, gestural remote control of synthesisers', which provides 'an interactive musical instrument destined for public use'.[51] He has also used it as 'a musical instrument accessible to the physically handicapped, an educational game for children, a creative game for the mentally handicapped'.[52]

There are, however, major differences between the two systems, which reflect their different starting points and the different intentions of their creators. The principal differences lie in their relative complexity, and their respective abilities as compositional tools in their own right. The Soundbeam system works linearly, like sonar. Each beam is independent and operates a different MIDI channel. What is happening to beam A does not affect what is happening to beam B.[53]

In Rolf Gehlhaar's 'Sound-Space', however, the beams are normally placed down two adjacent sides of a room, creating a grid that spans the space. Information from each beam is fed into a computer which reacts to the totality of information that it receives. The effect of this is that the entire space is mapped by the computer, and movement within the space is tracked and turned into sound. The space, then, becomes an instrument of considerable subtlety, which is capable of reacting to speed, for example. Running around the space will cause sounds very different from those made by a slow deliberate movement – just as hammering the keys of a piano will produce a different sound to gently stroking them. Moreover, the space can be divided into zones, each of which will trigger different sounds – which may be musical notes, unpitched noises or speech. The space will react to all movements within it, and so a group of people will create a different effect to a soloist.

If movement within a space creates sounds, and those sounds are patterned harmonically, then is the participant a dancer or a musician? Gehlhaar doesn't really mind how this question is answered, since he regards himself as 'a universalist working as a composer'.[54]

He has worked with dancers, however, to produce pieces which span both art forms. In 1986 he worked with Kilina Crémona to produce *Copernicopera*, which was devised and performed in Montpellier. In this a dance troupe triggers sounds as it moves around the courtyard of a castle. These sounds are reminiscent of an orchestra: an orchestra which does not exist but is danced into existence by the movement of the performers through the mapped space – performers who appear, to the audience, to be dancing in response to the music that they are in fact creating.

During the development of 'Sound-Space', Rolf Gehlhaar has attempted to involve a number of dancers and choreographers in the creation of dance/music pieces. As a result of this, he has come to a surprising conclusion: many dancers do not listen to music. They only listen to beats. He has come to believe that, for most dancers, the music they dance to is effectively no more than an elaborate metronome:

Dancers are not in the main used to listening to music. They are used to counting, but they are not at all used to reacting. They find this very difficult.[55]

In Gehlhaar's experience, dancers have found the idea that they might create an original piece of music by moving through an active space frightening, or baffling, or of little interest. In his view, only a very few dancers such as Laurie Booth or Jenny Jackson have really understood the potential of a system such as 'Sound-Space'. Most dancers do not seem to want the 'responsibility' of composing, even if they can do it by merely dancing.

In San Francisco, four women worked for a number of years on strategies to encourage people to use space to compose. These women were Candice Pacheco, Tina Blaine, Patti Clemens and Tina Phelps. They were members of the Underground Marimba Ensemble, and some of them were computer programmers. They wanted to make popular music.

We needed electronic percussion instruments that would give us the physicality of the Shona instruments and be able to have the incredible selection of sounds electronic music has to offer. Since what we were looking for wasn't available, and we were used to playing giant marimbas, we decided to create our own instruments.[56]

They named themselves D'Cuckoo,[57] and set about hand-building their own electronic instruments.

It wasn't like we each built our own though. We all spent so many sleepless nights soldering and trying to figure out how to hand-wire wrap our circuit boards… For two years we had less bugs and problems with those hand-wire wrapped boards than when we finally had the printed boards made. We had some really kinky problems with the printed boards. But the wire-wrapped ones, they were work horses.[58]

These instruments were not simply electronic marimbas. They wanted to use the possibilities of the digital realm to create instruments to let the audience join in their improvisations. They created the D'Cuckoo MIDI Ball™ which is 'a 5 foot wireless, clear, helium-filled sphere, stuffed with feathers, glitter, and a transmitter that triggers sound, light and video on-stage while the band keeps an infectious rhythm going'.[59] This ball is passed through the audience and, as it is bounced around, it triggers MIDI events, to which the band react. The events that the MIDI Ball triggers can be tailor-made to a specific occasion. When D'Cuckoo supported the Grateful Dead, for example, the Ball triggered samples of Jerry Garcia's singing.

Like David Jackson and Rolf Gehlhaar, their aim is to create spaces which are active – in which the audience is also a part of the orchestra.

Through using digital technology imaginatively, and bending it to their own particular needs, they are attempting to abolish the notion of the passive audience watching the active performer.

> We're greatly influenced by going to places like Africa where everyone is a musician, whether they are playing an instrument or not. Everyone is a part of whatever the festival or celebration is, and that kind of spirit is what we are trying to create at our shows.[60]

In different ways, all these musicians are working to create three-dimensional musically-active spaces, in which everyone present is necessarily involved as a creator.

12 *Sculpting in No-D*

It is late in 1989, and you are in Manhattan (or, possibly, you are in Amsterdam). You are sitting on a bicycle which is mounted on the floor. The room is dark, but in front of you words are projected onto a large video screen. As you pedal, you travel towards the words and past them, towards further words. When you turn the handlebars, the bicycle turns left or right, along other streets of words. The bicycle 'moves' through this imaginary city as quickly or as slowly as you pedal.

If you are observant, and if you are familiar with Manhattan or Amsterdam, you might eventually notice that the streets follow exactly the map of the city, and that the scale of the various letters and words conform to the scale of the buildings in those streets.

The Legible City was constructed by Jeffrey Shaw, an Australian artist who has been exploring multimedia since the 1960s. He was one of the first to build inflatable sculptures, and inflatable structures that people could walk round and through. He now lives in Amsterdam, and works digitally.

In the Manhattan version of the Legible City, the virtual space was 'based on the ground plan of part of Manhattan – the area boundaried by 34th and 66th Streets, and Park and 11th Avenues'.[61] The texts were written by Dirk Groenveld, and are a series of eight fictional monologues, by people ranging from Frank Lloyd Wright to a cab driver. Each story has a specific location in the city, and each is identified by lettering of a different colour. The cyclist can follow a single monologue through the city, or travel along any route, reading a collage of elements from the different stories.

Although what is happening is in reality no more than the projection of computer-generated images onto a large video screen, the effect of the experience can make it seem much more than that. It is easy to become involved in it, as the bicycle appears to carry you forward into the virtual environment. As with flight simulators, and other such computer-generated environments, the effect is immersive, with the result that disbelief is suspended and the illusion becomes momentarily convincing.

The Legible City enables the user to move through a space that does not exist; a place that bears a resemblance to somewhere we can know, but is in fact nowhere at all. Other artists are also working in this non-existent place. William Latham, for example, makes large sculptures in the Land of Nowhere. He spends much of his working time in a space that can never exist.

William Latham is a graduate of the Royal College of Art, who began his career by making conventional sculptures which could be exhibited in galleries. When experimenting with printmaking in 1984, he observed how the prints would change throughout an edition. This led him to create a large drawing called *The Evolution of Form*, which has a number of primitive geometrical shapes at the top: a cone, a cube, a sphere, a cylinder and a torus. These are altered by bulging, twisting or stretching as they are repeated down the picture. As a result they evolve into much more complex forms as they near the bottom of the drawing.

This led to a major shift in his interests.

> My focus of attention shifted from that of producing a single sculpture to the idea of producing millions of sculptures, each spawning a further million sculptures. The work of art was now the whole evolutionary tree of sculptures.[62]

His single-minded pursuit of this idea led him to be offered the post of Visiting Fellow at the IBM UK Scientific Centre in Winchester in 1987.

There he created sculptures 'by writing computer programs while sitting at a terminal looking at a computer screen'.[63] The program he used enabled him to type in a series of numbers which were used to 'seed' an evolutionary process. Each number described:

> a sculptural transformation such as the amount of 'twist' or 'stretch', or the number of primitives being 'unioned'. The larger the sequences of numbers passed to the evolution program the greater the complexity of the form which will be evolved. A sequence of parameters about the same length as a telephone number will create a form at the level of complexity of an egg with a horn growing out of it. By changing the parameters in the sequence the form is 'modified', by adding more parameters the form is 'evolved' into a more complex state.[64]

Latham's approach is to 'seed' a shape and then evolve it in numerous variations. Choosing the example that he likes best, he repeats the process by selecting one of the more complex shapes for further mutation. He continues to repeat this until he has a final shape that he likes, which he then works on in detail to produce a finished sculpture.

Rather than creating shapes, he claims to be discovering them. He has said that the computer 'has given me freedom to explore and create complex three-dimensional forms which previously had not been accessible to me, as they had been beyond my imagination'.[65]

Latham is insistent that 'what I am doing is sculpture and not computer graphics. It is three-dimensional work producing three-dimensional pieces.'[66] The pieces he 'evolves' are initially shown on the screen as wire-frame images. They can be viewed from any angle and at any distance. They can be rotated on the screen.

When William Latham has a shape he is happy with, he can create a texture which is then mapped onto the shape of the sculpture. He can vary the shininess, and the reflectivity of the material. He can make the surface smooth or ridged. When he has completed this he can shine imaginary lights onto the object, and then have the computer ray-trace the image to create light and shade, highlights and shadows.

He can then move the virtual camera, to view the sculpture from another angle – perhaps with different lighting. Latham believes that the computer print-outs that result are better thought of as photographs of three-dimensional objects that do not exist in our world, rather than as two-dimensional computer graphics. Many of these objects could not exist in the 'real' world because, inside the computer 'is a world free from physical constraints such as gravity, material resistance and time … Many of my sculptures float in space and are so intricate that they would be impossible to make.' [67]

His sculptures, however, 'exist' only mathematically. They have no real dimensions – all we can see are flat representations of them. He is sculpting in cyberspace, in No-D, a world of no 'actual' dimensions.

These sculptures have been documented in two forms. They exist as Cibachrome prints, some of which are as large as five feet square. Many of the sculptures also exist as video recordings. In these a virtual movie camera takes us on a voyage through galaxies of shapes, some of which revolve like planets, and some of which have moons in orbit around them. Some shapes are twisting, multicoloured tunnels which the camera enters and through which it glides. These films vary in length from 90 seconds to 30 minutes.

Recently William Latham has started to use his work for more commercial applications, although the nature of the work itself has not changed. In 1992 he founded Computer Artworks Ltd, which has begun work on computer games under the generic title *mind games,* as well as working videos such as the Shamen's single *Destination Eschaton.*

Latham's idea that art is discovered and not created is an ancient one, and he is following in a long tradition. Plato argued that reality 'consisted of pure essences or archetypal Ideas, of which the phenomena we perceive are only pale reflections. (The Greek word Idea is also translated as Form.) These Ideas cannot be perceived by the senses, but by pure reason alone.'[68]

The use of computers to explore objects in a computer-generated Land of Nowhere has helped revive a version of this tradition.

> The line between science and art is a fuzzy one ... Today computer graphics is one method through which scientists and artists reunite these philosophies by providing scientific ways to represent natural and artistic objects.[69]

The mathematics of fractals, popularised by Benoît Mandelbrot in his book *The Fractal Geometry of Nature,*[70] introduced the general public to a kind of computer-generated imagery which was breathtaking in its intricacy and beauty. These images were derived purely from mathematical equations describing patterns of fractals[71] and, depending on your point of view, their beauty was either natural or accidental. They also served to provide the manufacturers of posters and T-shirts with endless free designs, which they happily used.

> Fractals are characterised by a kind of built-in self-similarity in which a figure, the motif, keeps repeating itself on an ever diminishing scale. A good example is a tree with a trunk which separates into two branches, which in turn separate into two smaller side branches, and so on. In our mind we can repeat this an infinite number of times. The final result is a tree fractal with an infinite number of branches; each individual branch, however small, can in turn be regarded as a small trunk that carries an entire tree.[72]

In the medieval period the relationship between 'Idea' and 'Nature' was taken for granted, and geometry, and mathematical relationships such as the Fibonacci Series[73] and the Golden Section, were held to reveal divine truths. Buildings were constructed to reflect them, and they informed religious paintings. Piero della Francesca's *Baptism of Christ*, for example, 'follows the geometrical symbolism of the Golden Proportion as the Holy Trinity'.[74] The figures of Leonardo da Vinci also conform to geometric formulae.

William Latham has claimed that his work is 'dangerous. Some people actually find the images very disturbing.'[75] He believes this is because the sculptures that he 'evolves' mathematically are somehow archetypal, that they are variations of primary shapes which cannot but have a powerful psychological effect on us. He believes that these shapes reveal truths which, if not divine, are at least a glimpse of a fundamental part of nature.

From this perspective, William Latham, by working with numbers and the relationships they generate, is using modern tools to add to an ancient tradition. Using digital tools, the raw material upon which he works is the mathematics underpinning reality itself.

13 *Painting by numbers*

Painting digitally is literally painting with numbers: using a software package to create a file of noughts and ones which are interpreted by the computer as the instructions to display or print an abstract or representational image. Painting digitally can seem like child's play.

KidPix is a computer program, available for Macintosh or Windows-compatible computers, which is predicated on this assumption. Its success, and the fact that it has won at least nineteen awards, suggests that the assumption is true.

Using a simplified interface, children of four or five can happily create interesting patterns and paintings within a few minutes. At the same time the program is powerful enough to be usable by teenagers and adults. For some apparently adult tasks, such as the rapid creation of randomised backgrounds or textures for inclusion in a digital image, KidPix is the quickest and easiest program available.

For people engaged professionally in the creation of digital paintings, however, Adobe Photoshop is most usually the program of choice. Photoshop can be used for the electronic performance of traditional darkroom tasks such as enlarging or cropping images, removing scratches and dust marks from photographs, 'hand-tinting' black-and-white photographs, and dodging and burning parts of an image to make it lighter or darker. Many newspapers and magazines use so-called digital darkrooms for just these purposes.

However, Photoshop can also use a range of filters and effects to produce seamless montages. With a little careful effort, 'photographs' can be produced of an event that has never taken place.

In September 1993 newspapers around the world published an astonishing – almost unbelievable – photograph of [then] Israeli Prime Minister Yitzhak Rabin shaking hands with Palestine Liberation Organisation chairman Yasser Arafat on the White House lawn while President Bill Clinton looked on. In 1988 *Life* magazine published an equally striking picture of Chairman Arafat warmly greeting [the previous] Prime Minister Yitzhak Shamir under the approving gaze of President Ronald Reagan. One of these images recorded an actual event and provided reliable evidence that peace was perhaps at hand in the Middle East. The other was a computer-manipulated composite, a tongue-in-cheek fiction.[76]

Digital painting is causing many professional photographers a great deal of concern,[77] since it is having a direct effect on the idea that 'seeing is believing'; that photographs represent some kind of truth.

The provenance of a traditional photograph is often easy to trace, because exposed films, negatives and prints must be carried physically from place to place and because developing and printing must be performed in suitably equipped darkrooms. Digital image-making makes this job much tougher: it eliminates negatives, it can replicate files in seconds, and digital images can be transmitted rapidly and invisibly through computer and telephone networks.[78]

The erosion of the believability of photography is increasingly true in both the public and private spheres. There are now photographic studios where the divorced can have their old photograph albums digitally retouched to remove that embarrassing former spouse – or even have their current lover retrospectively inserted into their old snapshots.

Of course, in reality, photographs have *always* been constructed,[79] and have always involved at least some degree of manipulation; and an informed belief in their 'veracity' has always required a certain degree of technical sophistication. The roomful of Victorian 'spirit photographs' at the National Museum of Photography, Film and Television in Bradford provides evidence of this. Today almost all of these look like the amateurish double exposures that they were, but at the time they served to convince a lot of people of the existence of ectoplasmic ghosts and faeries.

Knowing that photographs can never be simply reflections of reality, some artists have embraced the tools available in the digital darkroom, to make original work which does not seek to disguise its artifice.

The Argentinian photographer Diego Goldberg has produced *Crónicas Apasionadas* (A Passionate Chronicle), which is a digital picture book celebrating his parents' seventieth birthdays. He mostly worked from original photographs which he scanned into a Macintosh computer. Many were enhanced, some were manipulated, and some were created on the computer.

One of the constructed images is of Perla, his mother, at work as a young woman at Kupfersmitt and Co. in Buenos Aires. No image of her at work existed. After some research the photographer found an image of an office from the same period and scanned that in alongside a *real* photograph of his mother taken at the same time. Both images were integrated by manipulating the tonality.[80]

Goldberg's mother thought the photograph was real when she saw it, and wondered how on earth he had managed to obtain it.

Goldberg used Photoshop to manipulate images in order to create pictures that might have been. Other photographers have used this kind of process deliberately to process images that could never exist in the real world.

Daniel Lee was born in 1945 in China, grew up in Taiwan, and took a Master's degree at Philadelphia College of Art. He now lives and works in New York City. Using a Hasselblad camera, an Apple Macintosh and a desktop scanner, he has created a series of 'manimals' – visual images that some people find intensely disturbing. One of them has recently been purchased by the Brooklyn Museum of Art.

The images are based on photographic portraits captured on 5 x 4 inch negatives. Each portrait is then manipulated using Photoshop's filters and brushes until the faces (although still recognisably human) have had their proportions altered so as to take on the characteristics of a particular animal. A Chinese man in a Mao suit looks like a human leopard. A man in a work shirt seems to be a horse. A woman in a black sweater looks like a snake. Another, who is semi-nude, resembles a cat.[81]

Although he works with animal reference books when he is composing his images, Lee makes no use whatsoever of superimposition or montage. Each image is created solely from one original photograph.

> For instance, take the face of a snake, it's so much flatter than a human's. It just wouldn't work to superimpose one on top of the other. I have to draw and paint each of the figures to ensure it looks realistic.[82]

The final images are printed out at 35 x 53 inches by an ink jet printer. Lee says,

> they aren't drawings, they aren't paintings and they aren't photographs. They are something entirely different created on the computer.[83]

Inez van Lamsweerde is a Dutch artist living and working in Amsterdam. She uses the same kind of Photoshop techniques but to deliberately shocking effect. Her series *Thank You, Thighmaster* consists of life-sized doll-women. These began with a series of photographs of female nudes. The images were produced by first digitally combining an image of a doll's head and each woman's face. This was done in such a way that the woman's face was replaced by the doll's face, but the 'skin' of the doll's face was then rendered with the texture of the woman's skin. Skin was then drawn over the nipples, and any trace of genitals was removed, to produce a disturbing toy-like effect, in which the hair, the muscle definition and the bone structure is too 'real' to be a doll, but the face is too doll-like to be a person.

This kind of work has become increasingly possible on even relatively cheap desktop computers. The cover CD-Roms that are mounted on the front of most computer magazines often contain collections of computer-generated — or manipulated images from professionals, from students and from hobbyists who happen to have access to the right software. Today, nothing is easier than placing your colleagues at work on the surface of Mars, or showing yourself on the beach with Clara Bow.

Digital imaging has now reached the point where, for the most part, technical wizardry has ceased to be interesting in its own right. Like any other images, it is the content, or the point of view of the image maker, that makes some digital imagery interesting.

Pete Dunn and Lorraine Leeson have worked in Docklands, in East London, for over twenty years – firstly as the Docklands Community Poster Project and latterly as the Art of Change. From the start they have used montage and collage to produce large billboards giving expression to community views. Originally they worked in the darkroom with a copy camera to enlarge images, and then on the floor of an old warehouse to collage the enlarged elements together onto boards which were then mounted onto the billboards.

Today they do almost all of their work on a suite of Apple Macintoshes, and almost all the collaging is done digitally in Photoshop. Pete Dunn believes,

> It's not the techniques themselves that are important. It's the fact that you can work faster and easier and, at the end of the day, you get better results. The computer doesn't work miracles. If the idea is no good then the finished result is no good. But if the idea is good, then the chances of the finished result being good are considerably better. You're no longer working against the odds all the time.[84]

In May 1995 the Art of Change completed a year-long project with the staff and students of George Green's School on the Isle of Dogs. This had been commissioned by the Tate Gallery and was designed to combine 'a critical studies approach to art appreciation together with practical work'.[85] During the project, a group of students recreated Stanley Spencer's painting of the Resurrection.

> The idea was to recreate Spencer's vision of an earthly paradise at Cookham in the Isle of Dogs. Changing the title to *Awakenings*, they set about transforming every detail of the painting.[86]

The students photographed themselves in the positions of the figures in Spencer's painting, and photographed the school and other local landmarks for the background. A montage was assembled on an Apple Macintosh using Photoshop. This process was complicated by the need to adjust the tonal and colour balances of the different components in order to ensure that the overall image was consistent. Elements also had to be scaled, and in some cases foreshortened, to achieve the required effects. Finally, a Cibachrome print of the montage was made which was 14 feet long and 7 feet high. This was exhibited at the Tate Gallery from May to October 1995.

From an entirely different perspective, Concept 3 Advertising in the USA also realised that digital images could be very interesting if they offered a unique point of view on a recognised topic. Concept 3 are the advertising agency responsible for selling us Absolut vodka. They regularly produce magazine advertisements which feature a picture of an Absolut bottle, with a two-word slogan such as *Absolut Attraction* or *Absolut Intelligence*. Although a few of these images are produced photographically, or by other means (one was a smudged photocopy of an Absolut bottle), most of them are digitally manipulated in some way, and the majority of them are created digitally.

A wide variety of people are commissioned to produce these advertisements (which appear, among other places, on the back cover of every issue of the American edition of *Wired* magazine). Because they are each trying to find a new way of presenting what is essentially the same image, they provide an interesting overview of the different approaches to digital creativity.

Jack Cliggett, the head of the Graphic Design Program at Drexel University, created one of the most visually arresting in the series. His version of the ad (the slogan of which is *Absolut Countryside*) shows a waterfall in the middle of some woods. The water appears to be pouring over the waterfall in the shape of an Absolut bottle, with the brand name just visible. He used two images: a picture of the waterfall and a picture of an Absolut bottle.

> He couldn't simply composite the two images, regulating the opacity of the transparent water and glass. He had to make the water flow over the physical structure of the supersize bottle.[87]

To do this he manipulated a series of images digitally, using Photoshop.

Painting digitally *is* child's play. It's painting by numbers. You just cause the computer to colour pixels, which are only dots on a screen. Doing it interestingly, however, is a creative challenge which requires some technical knowledge, but more importantly, a lot of imagination.

14 *Creative experiences in virtual galleries*

Twenty years ago Benson and Hedges revolutionised advertising with a series of surreal billboards and posters that made little or no mention of the product or product name, and strove towards the condition of art. Since then most other British cigarette advertising has followed their lead, as it has become increasing difficult, legally, to promote any virtues whatsoever in tobacco products. Unable or unwilling to extol the virtues and benefits of intoxication, the makers of Absolut vodka have followed the same route.

But, it might be asked, if these images are works of art, or acts of creative endeavour, should they not be on permanent display somewhere? The fact is, they are.

If you live in America, and you want to see the Absolut advertisements mounted like old masters on walls, you can go to the Absolut Museum.

> It is a totally unique 3-D computer program... The virtual hallways of Absolut Museum contain the images of over 200 photographs, paintings and fashion designs from the award winning advertising campaign. Walk through the main hallway and see the first Absolut Vodka advertisement, Absolut Perfection, or cross into Absolut Glasnost featuring the work of 26 talented Russian artists.[88]

There are two ways to go to the Absolut Museum – and you can do either without leaving home. You can dial a toll-free number and order a three-disk set for $29.95, or download a sample over the Internet, and then order the complete museum electronically. Access to the 'Museum' is therefore available both off-line and on-line.

The Absolut Museum is by no means the only virtual gallery that has been created, although it is the only one that has been created with the purpose of turning an advertising campaign into a cultural event. Many museums and galleries have begun to take tentative steps into cyberspace, some more wholeheartedly than others. A current list of these can be found at the Virtual Library museums page on the World Wide Web,[89] which is based at the University of Oxford. This provides direct links to several hundred galleries. Jonathan Bowen, the Virtual Library's administrator, thinks that the number of entries is currently doubling every three months as more and more institutions go on-line.

Probably the largest virtual gallery in the world is Le WebMuseum,[90] which is run by Nicholas Pioch, a multimedia consultant and teacher, in Paris. The WebMuseum was established in March 1994,[91] since when it has had over one and a half million visitors. Not only does it have large entries for many renowned artists but it also hosts special exhibitions and has won awards for its design and its depth of content.

The first 'real' museum in Britain to set up a Website of its own was the Natural History Museum. The site mirrors the structure of the museum itself. You move round a plan of the building, clicking on different galleries to visit them. Each gallery contains a set of graphics which try to give a flavour of the exhibition, together with accompanying text.[92]

Neil Thomson, who runs the Natural History Museum Website, does not think that it will affect attendances at the 'real' museum.

> People will always want to see the original of something they are interested in. What the Web should do is stimulate that interest by showing items that users may not have previously known were available.[93]

He believes,

> the Web is tailor-made to fulfil one of the museum's main objectives, which is to make information about the natural world available to as wide an audience as is humanly possible... Museums are the treasure houses of the nation and we are acutely aware that very little of what we have can be on public display. This is a way of opening up some of the material that would not normally be known about to a wide audience.[94]

Other institutions are beginning to think along the same lines.

Illuminations are a production company who have been very concerned with these issues, both in terms of producing television programmes like *The Net*, and within their multimedia work. Terry Braun, the head of Illuminations Interactive, was involved in creating a Website for the 1995 Turner Prize.

> In the end it was a PR device to draw attention to the Prize. It had pictures of the exhibits and text relating to the artists, but it was also

more than that. It was used heavily, and I suspect by many people who wouldn't necessarily have gone to the Tate – or maybe couldn't. And it provoked discussion on-line.[95]

Some small commercial galleries (mainly in America) have also started experimenting with adding a virtual wing on-line, often as part of a larger on-line virtual shopping mall. The Rhombus Gallery in Vermont is run by Matt Strauss and Mark Matt Harter, and they have a virtual wing[96] that you can walk around by clicking arrows on the edges of the screen. If you see a picture you like, you can click on it to find out more. You can order it electronically there and then, if you want to.

There are limitations to this kind of approach, however. At the best resolution that the Internet currently offers,

> the scanned-in, digitised images it makes available don't do justice even to the established works we're familiar with. In terms of image quality, they don't even reach the standards of the photographs in art books.[97]

Ordering an expensive watercolour solely on the basis of an image viewed on the Web, then, is much more than a mere purchasing decision. It is a new kind of gambling.

In view of this, the best prospect for virtual galleries seems to be virtual art. If something has been created on a screen, then presumably it can be viewed on a screen; and indeed many digital works are created specifically to be viewed on-screen.

The purest example of this kind of endeavour is the Genetic Art Gallery, run by John Mount at Carnegie Mellon.[98] This gallery is part of a research project concerned with the creation of images using evolutionary theory. In many ways the basis of this project is similar to the basis of William Latham's sculptural work. When you visit the site you are shown a range of images and invited to vote for your favourite. After every 10 votes a calculation is run automatically. On the basis of the votes it 'evolves' the next generation of images. Since November 1993, when the project began, it has 'evolved' in excess of eight thousand images. (You can order prints of any of these images that you particularly like, too!)

Other virtual galleries display changing exhibitions of digital art, which vary in quality. The University of Derby has a Digital Research Centre which runs what it terms The Virtual Gallery.[99] This has a wide range of exhibitions and events, including work by local artists. The Centre has developed a consultancy wing – DRC Internet. Together they have organised digital arts events such as *Feed Your Head* in February 1995 which, according to Geoff Broadway from DRC, aimed to 'create debate about the social implications of technology by bringing together a diverse range of practitioners from the realms of art, technology and digital culture.'[100]

There are many similar on-line galleries, with more appearing all the time. Pavilion in Brighton run the Pavilion Internet Gallery,[101] for example; while Joseph Squier of the School of Art and Design at the University of Illinois organises The Place.[102] This site is a serious attempt to do more than just display digital work. It is an attempt to begin to explore digital aesthetics, and to use the Web to discover what creativity is and how it works.

We should not be surprised that digital galleries are appearing on a daily basis, and under all sorts of pretexts. Desktop publishing made it possible for a great many people to produce a reasonable looking booklet, and on the basis of this a number of people (including Ted Nelson) turned to self-publishing – something they would never even have considered 10 years previously. The World Wide Web makes it possible for a great many people to publish on-line at a fixed cost of £15 to £20 per month, and as the effective costs continue to drop we should expect to see ever more of them. Some of them will have the charm (or complete lack of charm) of any kind of vanity publishing. Some of them will be important and influential.

Virtual galleries and museums will be as interesting, entertaining and useful as the ideas behind them. The fact that a gallery is deemed important in the 'real' world is no guarantee that its 'on-line wing' will be of any interest whatsoever. If its purpose is vague, its content poor, and its design dull, then people will pass it by.

Virtual exhibitions will succeed when they are powered by a clear set of ideas, properly realised. These ideas can be commercial, experimental, aesthetic, moral or anti-commercial. The Absolut Museum works because its designers knew what it was supposed to do, and it does it. The Place works because it is run with a clear purpose in mind. The Genetic Art site works because as soon as a user visits the site they become part of the ongoing experiment, and the ongoing experiment also happens to be entertaining *and* visually interesting. Could you resist visiting again to see what effect your vote had on the evolution of the imagery?

15 *Digital experiences in the real world*

While some institutions are making moves into cyberspace, still others are beginning to stage digital work in their traditional spaces.

Artists such as Jenny Holzer have worked in this way for a long time. Her continuing interest is the ambivalence of aphorisms in the public sphere, and the ways in which slogans are received and interpreted. She began in 1979 by posting cryptic messages on walls all over New York City. Since then she has used electronic noticeboards and advertising hoardings to house her slogans, as well as printing them on clothing. Recently she created a piece called *World II*, a virtual reality installation for the Guggenheim Museum in SoHo, New York, which was viewed through a virtual reality headset.

In this piece a group of villagers describes its experiences of the aftermath of an unspecified war in cryptic and allusive terms.

> It was clear that the strategies used in Bosnia are all-too-common techniques of war, so I thought about how to translate this sort of content into a VR world, and it seemed that it would be much more immediate if the material was spoken by men and women rather than printed out.[103]

The virtual world she created was very static. The user walks through a landscape, in and out of buildings; and in each building somebody gives their testimony. Holzer claims that this apparent restriction was by deliberate choice, and not through any limitations in the technology. 'So much of art-making is about reducing things to the essentials... I don't want it to look natural because then I would be making a documentary film.'[104]

Holzer has a clear purpose in creating a virtual reality inside a 'real' space,

> trying to make life seem real enough that one is moved to do something about the more atrocious things. By going really far afield into a completely fake world, maybe there's a chance to make things resonate somehow.[105]

In creating this piece Holzer worked with programmers from Sense8 and scientists from Intel. She does not believe that there is a fundamental difference between 'artists' and 'scientists'. 'Not to sound like a multidisciplinary dweeb, but there really is an artificial line between someone who is a real artist and someone who is writing the software for the stuff.'[106]

People in Britain are also working to explore the common ground between artists and scientists. The Arts Catalyst was conceived in July 1993 by Nicola Triscott and Vivienne Glance, and began work in earnest in the spring of 1995. Their aims are twofold. Firstly, they believe that although artists and scientists habitually 'think and plan in such different ways'[107], they can usefully and practically learn from each other. Secondly, their experience has led them to believe that artists and scientists, encouraged to work together, can produce very interesting work – work that neither group would produce on its own.

They agree with Jenny Holzer that artists need to take computer programming seriously if they are to work digitally.

> Interactivity is what is exciting artists. They are concerned with the human/technological interface. They want to get physical involvement and emotional involvement.[108]

As part of their Supernova science-art project, they commissioned Simon Robertshaw and Sinclair Stammers to work with Dr Chris Stringer and Dr Duncan Gillies from Imperial College and the Natural History Museum, to produce a 'huge interactive video and computer installation at the Natural History Museum in July and August 1955,[109] entitled *The Nature of History*.

The installation was in a side gallery on the ground floor of the museum. It attracted a range of viewers, some of whom (perhaps inevitably) simply wandered in, looked around, puzzled, and wandered out again. The gallery contained videos of hugely magnified organisms, projected onto the floor, along with wall-mounted still images. The highlight of the exhibition, however — in terms of user involvement — was undoubtedly the large interactive piece at the far end of the gallery, in which huge projected images changed according to the human movement in front of them.

> The intelligent camera set-up that facilitates viewer interaction in the *Nature of History* exhibition is an example of the emerging technology called computer vision: a subject of research for around thirty years,

whose applications in medicine, robotics and, more ominously, surveillance and the military are becoming increasingly known.[110]

The camera locked onto a single person moving inside a grid in front of the screens and altered the displays according to their movement. If they stood still for too long, then the camera locked onto the movements of another person, and tracked them until they too stood still.

The exhibition created a revealing array of responses. On the time I visited the exhibition with my ten-year-old son, the intelligent camera was the continual source of attraction for groups of children, who would come in and interact with it for up to thirty minutes. The response of many adults to it was much more hesitant and much more guarded. The parties who stayed longest in the exhibition were almost invariably those with one or more children.

Afterwards, I purchased a catalogue from the bookshop. The man who served me asked what I had thought of the exhibition, and then said 'I don't really understand it myself.' This echoed the response of the woman on the information desk where I had asked about the location of the exhibition. She had raised her eyebrows and pointed. 'It's down there, if you can make anything of it.' As we left the bookshop my son turned to me and said, 'Is there supposed to be something you have to understand? Don't you just go in there and play until you've had enough, and then leave?'

The idea of experiencing an event without trying to 'decode' it is very familiar to children and young people who have grown up with Nintendos and Megadrives. Playing the *Super Mario* games, for example, mostly involves finding out what the rules governing the play are – through trial and error, or by swapping information with friends. The storylines are almost non-existent, and are there solely to provide some sort of communicable goal for the activity. The characters are a motley assortment of Italian plumbers, armour-plated turtles, rhinos and worms, alongside a Princess and a gorilla named Donkey Kong.

Much of Jenny Holzer's work also depends on the fact that it is impossible to decode material which is deliberately ambiguous or opaque. She makes use of the paraphernalia of digital life to do this, by constructing displays that mimic advertising in both form and content. Simon Poulter is an English artist who has also explored the possibilities of using the digital environment to create work which comments on that environment, making sharp cultural and political arguments. Poulter is a conceptual artist based in Bridport in Dorset, who has become interested in digital technology. In 1994 he was commissioned by Hull Time Based Arts to create a work as part of its *Propaganda* series.

Poulter conceived UK Ltd – a work intended to 'expose the flaws and inconsistencies of the so-called free market. The work utilised technology throughout, as a way of reducing costs and facilitating the flow of information.'[111]

The intention of the work was 'to run a PR and marketing campaign in the manner of British Airways or British Gas'[112] and to this end prospectuses, advertising and press releases were produced. In addition, a website was established for UK Ltd. A pathfinder prospectus was published, offering a complete portfolio of deregulated services, in order to encourage investors. The establishment of a theme park at Stonehenge was planned in detail and publicised. As a result of this, Poulter was interviewed on Radio Four and appeared at the Conservative Party conference, as well as receiving considerable local and national press coverage.

The use of digital technology to run the UK Ltd campaign meant:

> a major national publicity campaign could be run from one computer using a database of contacts and a bank of images created in Photoshop which the press regarded as sexy. We were able to take on the media at their own game.[113]

Poulter regarded the use of the Internet as important because it enabled him to reach people who would normally never come into contact with his work. As a result of the success of the UK Ltd website, he is planning further projects involving use of the Internet.

> Those interested in following the story should look out for further products which will be unveiled in 1996, including The National Museum of Scratchcards, which will display the earliest known Gutenberg Scratchcard dating back to 1452.[114]

Like Jenny Holzer's pieces, Simon Poulter's work exists in real space but gains its resonance from its appropriation of features of the digital landscape. However, he has arguably gone one stage further by successfully creating work which, although 'real', nonetheless manifests itself digitally. In doing this, he has begun to use the Internet as a medium of creative expression.

In this he is far from alone. Jake Tilson has worked for several years at the

Laboratory at the Ruskin School of Art and Design, in Oxford, which was 'conceived as a think-tank for art where the right and duty to experiment is upheld'.[115] There he has created *The Cooker*, a rich and complex website with three distinct areas.[116] This is intended both as a repository of his past work, and as an arena for the creation of work specifically intended to use the Internet as a medium of expression. *The Cooker* is graphically rich and designed for non-linear exploration; its contents range from *What is Not a City?* to a fortune cookie game.

The Australian artist Simon Biggs, well-known for his digital installations, has also begun working on-line.[117] He is concerned, however, that the interactive nature of his work is not limited to the standard 'interaction' of computer games: 'for me the main point of interactivity is relations between people, not relations between people and machines'.[118]

Biggs' work draws heavily on the history of art, and the rich language of medieval religious iconography. It refuses to use computers for their own sake, and thus avoids generating digital clichés: effects that are used simply because the computer can produce them.

In a very individual way Biggs, like the others mentioned in this chapter, is grappling with the difficult problem of producing work which is rich in content, genuinely non-linear and yet still capable of producing emotional and intellectual resonances in the user which relate to experience in the real world.[119]

16 *Bits of language*

Not every activity that is normally categorised as part of 'the arts' will be affected by the digital revolution in the same way, or to the same extent. In many ways, the degree to which any creative activity is likely to be affected will depend on how many people are traditionally involved, and how much equipment is used in the processes of production and distribution.

A production of Wagner's *Ring Cycle* and a traditional Morris dance can both be described as pieces of musical theatre, but there are vast differences between them. The production of the former will involve several hundred highly trained people rehearsing in a large, specially designed space for several weeks, while the production of the latter will require only eight or nine people, some bells and sticks, an accordion, an open space, and several gallons of beer.

In this respect, writing can be likened to Morris dancing. It need involve little more than a human being, a writing implement, some paper and creative ingenuity. For this reason, it has always been possible, within the realms of literature, to stretch or twist linear forms in order to construct apparently non-linear works.[120]

In the eighteenth century Laurence Sterne attempted just such a thing in the book *Tristram Shandy*, which began with a long monologue from the eponymous unborn baby, and included blank and half-finished pages. In the early years of the twentieth century, following in the footsteps of abstract painters, many different writers began experimenting with ways in which linearity could be transcended.

On 25 June 1917, Hugo Ball (Dadaist and founder of the Cabaret Voltaire) introduced 'a new art form in which Ball carried his quarrel with language to its logical conclusions'.[121] He had written in his diary that the 'next step is for poetry to discard language as painting has discarded the object, and for similar reasons',[122] and so he gave a public performance of his first abstract phonetic poem, entitled *O Gadji Beri Bimba*. The shockable were, needless to say, shocked.

The Dadaist Tristan Tzara also sought to move beyond the 'tyranny of thought' in his writing. He adopted a different strategy, seeking

> to follow the principle of chance to its logical or illogical conclusion in literature. Sounds are relatively easy to put together, rhythmically and melodically, in chance combinations; words are more difficult. Words carry a burden of meaning designed for practical use, and do not readily submit to a process of random arrangement. It was however exactly this that Tzara wanted. He cut newspaper articles up into tiny pieces, none of them longer than a word, put the words in a bag, shook them well, and allowed them to flutter onto a table.[123]

The result of this process was deemed to constitute a poem, and to reveal something of the personality or mood of the poet who created it.

James Joyce made considerably more laborious attempts to move beyond the linear narrative, with its fixed point of view. Joyce's concerns were increasingly with the non-linear, the 'coincidental'. He was concerned with using narrative to create a multiplicity of meanings. Almost every word in *Finnegans Wake* has more than one meaning, or more than one point of reference, and the structure of the novel is itself circular. The famous first sentence of the novel,

> riverrun, past Eve and Adam's, from swerve of shore to bend of bay, brings us by a commodius vicus of recirculation back to Howth Castle and Environs.

is, in fact, the concluding half of the sentence that finishes the novel,

> A way a lone a last a loved a long the

Robert Anton Wilson has written,

> Perhaps no novelist in history has been as concerned with synchronicity as James Joyce ... When James Joyce feared that he might die without finishing *Finnegans Wake*, he selected Robert Stephens to complete it, not on any literary grounds per se, but because Stephens was born on the same day as Joyce (2 February 1882) and in the same city (Dublin) – and also because Stephens had the same first name as Joyce (James) and had a last name that differed by only one letter from the first name of Stephen Dedalus, Joyce's self-caricature in *A Portrait of the Artist as a Young Man* and *Ulysses*.[124]

Joyce's concerns were not purely 'literary' then, in a conventional sense. They were much broader than that. As Samuel Beckett once wrote,

> To Joyce reality was a paradigm, an illustration of a perhaps unstatable rule. It is not a perception of order or of love, it is a perception of coincidence.[125]

Exploring the powers of coincidence, and evoking the use of chance as a co-author, has been a pressing concern to many twentieth-century writers. In the 1950s, in Tangiers, William Burroughs and Brion Gysin experimented with 'cut-ups' in a way that bore remarkable similarities to Tristan Tzara's escapades. Burroughs wrote laconically,

> The method is simple. Here is one way to do it. Take a page. Like this page. Now cut down the middle and across the middle... Now rearrange the sections placing section four with section one and section two with section three. And you have a new page.[126]

This methodology became a cornerstone of his writing in books like *The Naked Lunch*.

The poet Spike Hawkins attempted something similar in the late 1960s, again reworking Tzara's idea. *Instant Poetry Broth* was a polythene package filled with small cards containing evocative phrases and words which could be arranged in any order to form poems. For example,

> I sat on the shelf
> I rule
> The lost fire brigade
> For the sake of my health

In 1969 the English novelist BS Johnson wrote a book which was designed to be read in almost any order. *The Unfortunates* was published in a box which contained 27 separately bound sections. One was marked as the beginning, and one was marked as the end. The reader was invited to shuffle the other 25 sections into a random order before reading the book.

In a similar vein, Alan Ayckbourn and other playwrights have experimented with devising plays with two or more alternative endings, decided in some experiments by the audience voting in the interval, and in others by devices such as one of the actors tossing a coin during a scene in the penultimate act.

Attempts like this, however, were not altogether successful; nor could they be. They are the equivalent of watching a magician performing a trick while explaining how it is done. The reader can see that Johnson's book has 27 sections, and can quickly intuit how limited the apparent randomness really is. Similarly, the reader can read all of Hawkins' cards separately and then fail to be surprised or excited by any of the 'random' poems that later reveal themselves. As with the games books of Steve Jackson and Ian Livingstone, readers can simply override the non-linearity and cheat, retracing any paths they have taken which led to an early bath, and trying again and again until they get it 'right'.

Digital systems, on the other hand, are inherently non-linear, and the cultural products of these systems can carry that non-linearity with them. If *The Unfortunates* had been produced as a floppy disk or CD-Rom then the reader would have seen the trick but not found the explanation of how it was done.

Indeed if BS Johnson were alive to produce work digitally he would undoubtedly realise that the idea behind the work could be extended infinitely further than the format of a book would ever allow. There could be hundreds of separate sections, and the ways in which they were linked could be as complex as the author required. It would be possible, for example, to arrange that the order in which the work was read determined whether or not several characters appeared at all and what the outcome was. In other words, it would be possible to have a dozen different final sections, and use the order in which the work was perused to determine which one was shown each time.

Michael Joyce, the co-ordinator of the Centre for Narrative and Technology at Jackson Community College, Michigan, has published just such a work, *Afternoon, A Story*, using a software package he helped develop called StorySpace.

> Many of *Afternoon*'s pages end with a question addressed directly to the reader, usually taking the form of 'Do you want to hear more about this?' A 'yes' will continue the narrative in similar vein, while a 'no' will send the story off on a new tangent.[127]

The 'book' is written in a truncated and experimental style, however, which is either a portent of new developments or an easy way of cheating.

Many of the interesting discussions that have arisen around hypertext as a literary medium are concerned with the perceived problems of maintaining an authorial view in a multidimensional text. If the reader can make Macbeth decide that murder is, after all, out of the question, then what is the point of the story? If Lady Macbeth suffers no guilt, and the 'damned spot' turns out to be merely a gravy stain, then what is the moral?

In these circumstances there is a real possibility that a story will descend into nothing more than a series of sequential events. By writing *Afternoon, A Story* in the style he does – a style which 'is fairly experimental and would have remained disconcertingly non-linear had it been published in book form',[128] Joyce neatly evades this issue.

The Spot is a relatively new website[129] which attempts to deal head-on with at least some of the problems of maintaining an authorial view in a multidimensional text. The site is an expensively produced ongoing soap opera, which *Internet* magazine has described as 'a cross between *Melrose Place* and MTV's *Real World*'. The saga began on 6 June 1995 with a pilot episode, and new episodes are produced daily. It is concerned with the trials and tribulations of seven young Californians[130] and their dog Spotnik, but the story is not presented linearly. There is no single narrative. Instead the site contains regularly updated letters, diary entries, and photographs, as well as biographies of each of the characters. The entries can be perused in whole or in part, and in any order. Often, the narratives provided by different characters give completely different perspectives on the same (fictional) events.

The Spot is not intended primarily as a literary endeavour. It is joyfully populist and commercial: as closely related to *Baywatch* as it is to *Citizen Kane*. Nevertheless, it provides an interesting and exciting example of an attempt to render narrative in a non-linear way – as a kind of episodic, fragmented but patterned mosaic.

It also provides a clear example of a large company undertaking a development project aimed at exploring some of the creative consequences of the new digital methods of publishing and distributing entertainment.

17 *No paper please, we're digital*

In 1994, for the first time, more personal computers were sold in the USA than televisions. It has been estimated that at least 70 per cent of these were equipped to use CD-Roms. Although there is, as yet, no single standard for electronic publication (what is playable on one computer is not necessarily playable on another), CD-Roms have begun to be perceived as a mainstream publishing activity.

CD-Roms enable information to be delivered easily and cheaply in very large chunks. A CD-Rom can hold up to 650 megabytes of data in the form of text, pictures, speech, music, sounds and movies. If a CD-Rom held only text files, it could contain over 110 million words.

Once the material for a CD-Rom has been assembled, pressing the physical discs is a process similar to pressing an audio compact disc. The costs are approximately equivalent. At 5,000 units the cost of pressing discs falls to less than £1 each. The warehousing and distribution costs involved in selling 110 million words on one disc need be no more than those of the latest Michael Jackson record, and are therefore considerably less daunting than the thought of storing and marketing the same number of words bound in several dozen large hardback books.

Large publishing companies like Dorling Kindersley in Britain and Voyager in the USA are producing increasing amounts of electronic publications in the fields of information, education and instruction, and entertainment. Dorling Kindersley were acclaimed in late 1995 for producing a stunning version of *The Way Things Work*. Voyager, who are regarded by many as the pioneers in the field, have produced a range of publications ranging from the pioneering *Beethoven's Ninth* to the *Residents' Freak Show*.

Voyager have also produced a series of 'expanded books', which include the texts of previously printed books made available on floppy disks, often with additional features. These have included three of William Gibson's cyberspace novels, as well as non-fiction works such as *The InterNet Companion* by Tracy Laquey and Jeanne C. Ryer. They are designed to be read on laptop, as well as desktop, computers.

Many traditional publishers are now abandoning their scepticism of paper-free publishing, and starting electronic divisions. The 1995 Frankfurt Book Fair had two halls devoted solely to electronic publishing, with almost four hundred exhibitors. Those exhibiting included large international mainstream publishing houses such as Bertelsmann, Random House and Marshall Cavendish.

In early 1995, Andreas Whittam Smith, founder and former editor of the *Independent*, sold his shares in the newspaper's parent company to the Mirror Group in order to finance the establishment of Notting Hill Multimedia, in partnership with his son Ben. Whittam Smith believes that there will be a bright future for multimedia publications 'which are not simply a rehash of old books, but are thought through properly, and designed to take full advantage of the possibilities of the medium'.[131] Notting Hill Multimedia currently has four CD-Roms in production. One is *The Which? Wine Guide*, to which Whittam Smith has bought the CD-Rom publishing rights. The other three are explorations of classical singing, the history of athletics, and the theory of evolution. These are all intended for an international audience.

The nature of creating CD-Roms is such that the largest production cost is time. One person, working on their own with a scanner, a desktop computer, the right software, a huge hard disk, a good idea and a lot of imagination, could produce a CD-Rom of the highest quality. With the current technical limitations a single creator could produce a work which would bear comparison with the best that is currently available. They could do everything that Dorling Kindersley could do – it would just take them a considerably longer time.

Peter Small is just such a creator. He first became obsessed with the possibilities of the new medium in 1988. The following year he took a small stand at the MacUser Show to launch Genome. At that point he had no finance, and no CD-Roms. All he had was an idea, and an evangelical leaflet promoting it. He took the names and addresses of anyone who showed any interest in his ideas, and began mailing them. His first mailing said that the Genome 'project is about developing a forum which will enable us to teach and inspire each other'.

The project changed as it developed and in 1992 Genome released its first CD-Rom entitled *Does God Make God?* This explored number theory and philosophy in a way which was entertaining, illuminating and utterly idiosyncratic. It received excellent reviews and went on to sell very respectably. It had been made entirely by Peter Small himself, exploring his personal obsessions and working at home. Other than several years of his time, the production costs were negligible.

The future of electronic publishing by means of CD-Roms is not entirely rosy, however. In the last twelve months a number of major publishers have retrenched or gone out of business. In America, Mammoth Micro Productions was shut down by its major shareholder, the *Washington Post*, for example, while MDI and Attica Cybernetics both went out of business.

This has happened while the amount of CD-Rom players bought and owned has continued to increase rapidly. As Andreas Whittam Smith has noted,

> the European markets are expanding very rapidly. Some of the richer markets, like Scandinavia, have a very high penetration of home PCs. In the US between 9 and 13 million households have installed CD-Roms. In Germany it is 1.2 million; in the UK it will reach a million this Christmas.[132]

Analysts have argued about this apparent contradiction. Writing in *Interactive Media International*, Tony Feldman has claimed,

> the apparent speed of growth of the title market has provoked the worst excesses of competitive pressure – wildly spiralling production budgets driven higher by the insane belief that more money spent means a better, more saleable product; suicidal price cuts in a desperate bid to secure volume sales and heavy over-publishing without real understanding of the nature of the consumer demand underpinning the still embryonic market.[133]

Publishers have been churning out titles in the belief that the company with the biggest backlist will be most likely to attract mass sales, without stopping to ask why anybody at all would ever want to buy a recipe book which had to be loaded onto a computer to be read. Or why anybody would want to read *Zen and the Art of Motorcycle Maintenance* on a train by draining the batteries of their Powerbook, rather than by thumbing through the paperback – especially since in almost every case the paperback is less than half the price of the 'expanded book'.

This problem has been compounded by the fact that there are no clear distribution channels, or retail outlets, for CD-Roms. If I want an interactive cookery book on CD-Rom, where will I find it? In the cookery section of my local computer shop? Somewhere in the basement of a record shop? In the computer section of my local bookshop?

It is most unlikely that many computer retailers are going to invest in the amount of stock that would be necessary to transform themselves into fully-fledged electronic bookshops, unless they receive clear indications that this move will be profitable. So far there are no such indications with the inevitable result that, in all but a few cases, CD-Roms have to be ordered. This, in turn, reduces to something approaching zero the chance of potential customers browsing and making impulse purchases.

For this reason, many electronic publishers are beginning to explore on-line publishing – distributing material over the Internet. There is currently a lot of argument about the safety of financial transactions over the Internet, and about whether or not on-line publication will create the possibility of mass piracy. There are suggestions that both of these problems can be eliminated though the use of encryption.[134]

A growing number of newspapers and magazines are establishing on-line editions. Most of these are free to the user and are intended to pay for themselves through the inclusion of advertisements. They usually include some or all of the printed version of the magazine, together with some exclusive material, often consisting of updates to printed articles, or lengthier versions of them.

Wired magazine has adopted an interestingly different approach. It publishes an electronic companion called *HotWired*.[135] From the outset this 'was staffed with entirely new (and younger) journalists and technologists, housed in separate offices and designed to appeal to a different demographic to the print magazine'.[136] The owners of *Wired* recognised from the beginning that the kind of people who currently use the Internet are likely to differ from the readers of traditional print magazines, and acted accordingly.

HotWired has rapidly achieved international popularity both for its content and its design, and is regarded as proof that webzine publishing is genuinely feasible. It is intended that it will become profitable through selling advertising space, rather than charging users to access it. In the last twelve months its advertising revenue was approximately $1.7 million, which meant that it almost covered its costs.

This kind of electronic publication has proved particularly useful to smaller magazines, and especially to those magazines which are published for love, or out of personal obsession, rather than with any realistic hope of making large amounts of money. In the last decade the falling costs of desktop publishing tools, and their growing ease of use, have made possible large numbers of 'zines' and newsletters dealing with topics ranging from poetry and general arts, to club culture, football, science fiction, satire and personal abuse. Many of these are now producing on-line versions, and an increasing number are switching entirely to on-line publication.[137] The primary reasons for this are the decrease in distribution costs and the possibility of gaining an international audience.

bOING bOING, for example, is a quarterly magazine that was established in 1988 by Carla Sinclair and Mark Frauenfelder. They decided that the first issue of 1996, will be their last paper-based issue. It will then continue as a website.[138] This will be updated regularly and will contain the kind of interactive discussion groups that are not possible in a quarterly magazine. In Mark Frauenfelder's words, their reasons for switching to digital publication are that 'Carla and I can no longer handle the burden of printing, distributing, and fulfilling subscriptions for 17,500 copies an issue. Doing a website makes all those problems go bye bye!'[139]

Rebel Inc. is a magazine based in Edinburgh, and edited by Kevin Williamson. It has fused the local rave and poetry scenes to produce a hard-hitting magazine featuring Scottish writers such as Irvine Welsh, Alison Kermack and Alan Warner. In December 1995 they produced their final printed edition, and launched their new on-line edition.[140] The first on-line edition contains pieces from the previous printed issues, although it is intended that future editions will contain original and commissioned material. Williamson also intends the website to have hypertext links into a *Rebel Inc.* newsgroup where public debate can take place, as well as having a monthly real-time discussion with at least one of the authors.

The major disadvantage of following this route is self-evident. An electronic zine will be able to reach only those people who have access to the Internet, and who know where to look for it, and this is a relatively narrow self-selecting group of people. Some publishers, including Andreas Whittam Smith, are therefore seeking to develop a hybrid solution. All Notting Hill Multimedia's work will be distributed on CD-Rom, since he believes that, for the present at least, this is the way he will reach the widest audience. Each disc, however, will contain specially designed software which, on request, will search the Internet for updates to the information on the disc, which it will then place in a folder on the user's hard disk.

In theory, then, a publication such as *The Which? Wine Guide* need never go out of date. For many (but not all) users, addenda and updates will be merely a local phone call away. Whittam Smith believes that new editions of the CD-Rom will continue to sell, however, because sooner or later it will seem like a good idea to most regular users to tidy up all the appendices, updates, and addenda lying in folders on their hard disks, by buying a later edition that incorporates these into the information on the disc itself.

An annual edition of the CD-Rom will have the same sort of status as books like the *Guardian Bedside Reader* which gather into a single easy-to-use reference book information which would otherwise be stored separately or lost. For this approach to succeed it will be important that the content is successfully organised and designed in such a way that the user feels comfortable with it as an on-screen work of reference.

18 *A screen is not a page*

The economics of electronic publishing may or may not be attractive, and there may or may not be an audience out there waiting for electronic publications. One thing *is* certain, however. There is still no consensus about what kind of thing a CD-Rom actually is, about what one should look like when it is loaded into the computer, and about how it should be used.

Frank Boyd is the director of Artec, which was established in Islington four years ago to fuse arts, design and computing skills and to harness these for vocational training. Artec have worked with galleries and museums including the Tate and the V&A, as well as producing·commercial work. Their trainees have gone on to work for the Multimedia Corporation, Dorling Kindersley, ITN, NoHo Digital and other companies.

In Boyd's words,

> professionals have developed clear ideas about the kind of budgets you need to make a film or a television series. Traditional publishers know what kind of advances they should expect to offer. With CD-Roms people are still working in the dark. If you think of them as books that do a bit more, then you will expect to work with an increased book budget. If you think of them as movies on disk, then you will expect an entirely different scale of production costs. The odd thing is that both approaches are possible, and both approaches can work.[141]

To a large extent the divergence in approaches is not merely economic, but also conceptual. Electronic publishing can be seen as a new mechanism for delivering traditional material with some peripheral enhancements. Alternatively it can be seen as the beginning of an entirely new medium of expression, with its own unique potential.

The designers of many electronic encyclopedias and reference books have taken the former approach. Existing text and illustrations are placed on-screen, and enhanced with database-like search engines which enable the user to find, for example, every occurrence of the word 'London' in one step. However, unless the value added by these alleged enhancements is sufficient to justify switching on the computer, loading the CD-Rom and then sitting two feet away from a screen for a couple of hours, this approach raises an obvious question: wouldn't I be better off with a book from a shelf?

It is sometimes possible for this approach to justify itself. An American publication, *The Home Repair Encyclopedia*, is a sophisticated CD-Rom which provides a multitude of different ways of accessing the information on the disc as projects, reference guides, cross-linked explanations of how a house works, tool-specific instructions and tips, survival guides, and estimators to assist in planning projects. Each of these approaches to the information has been designed to facilitate a particular kind of task. In order to do this, the information has not simply been replicated from a printed book. It has been fundamentally reconceived as semi-detached modules which can be assembled like building blocks into different shapes – with each shape making seamless sense.

This approach is fraught with design difficulties, not least of which is that several hundred years of literacy has trained us to think of information linearly. After all, what is 'alphabetical order' except a predictable linear progression learned so early in life that it becomes taken for granted?

Terry Braun, the head of Illuminations Interactive, believes that we are witnessing the beginning of an entirely new medium of expression:

> There are three major problem areas as far as the design of electronic multimedia is concerned: the content, the design of individual screens, and the interface, the way you find your way through the thing. A lot of the CD-Roms I have seen are really just a lot of linear content that tries to look as though it's somehow non-linear.[142]

The problem here is that traditionally, design occurs after the work has been created. Writers finish their work, editors amend it, and it is then passed to the designer. In most magazines, for example, the only design criterion that is applied before the piece is written concerns the length of the article: that is, the size of the hole in the magazine that it is intended to fill.

This works successfully only because a lot of the fundamental design criteria have already been taken care of by several hundred years of cultural conditioning. The designer will assume that the text will be linear – that the second paragraph will follow the first, and that there will be a final paragraph which will go at the end. She or he will assume that the reader will recognise the large type at the top of the page as a headline, and then assume that the first paragraph under the headline in the left-hand column is the start of the article. She or he will assume that the reader will automatically move from the bottom of page 16 to the top of page 17.

In an electronic publication that aims to be interactive and non-linear, this will simply not be the case. A screen is not a page. There is not necessarily only one 'next screen': it may be possible to travel to several destinations from any one starting point. It may be possible to arrive at a screen of information from several completely different starting points.

In order for the many routes through such a piece all to work seamlessly, the relationship between the author and designer may need to move away from the models used in traditional publishing. It may need to become more like the relationship between a screenwriter and film director, where the screenplay is rewritten or amended while the film is being shot because the consequences of shooting a scene in one particular way means that the following scene will no longer work in its original form.

Philip Ellington is a graphic designer who heads Strategic Design. He also chairs MacUniversity, a leading training agency for Apple Macintosh applications. He says,

> MacUniversity began five years ago as a self-help group for designers who were beginning to work electronically. Because of this, we have always been as concerned with the design aspects as with the business of mastering specific applications. One of the things that has become very clear to us is that people use information presented on computers very differently from the way they would use the same information presented on paper.
>
> People come to computers with an entirely different set of expectations from those they bring to a book. They often bring expectations from watching television or from what they feel – positively or negatively – about video games. They expect on-screen information to be user-friendly, and if it is not they rapidly lose interest.[143]

There is no traditional grammar for designing screens in the way that there is for designing pages, and no consensus about what constitutes user-friendliness. Many designers have built interfaces for their work that attempt to be friendly by virtue of their familiarity. They deliberately ape the standard Macintosh or Windows interface using labelled buttons of a standard size and shape, pop-up menus, scrolling lists and dialog boxes.

Ellington believes that this kind of design will ultimately be self-defeating:

> The on-screen equivalent of Roneoed newsletters simply announces to any potential user that the product is dull.

Caroline Grimshaw of Two-Can Publishing, who are responsible for the design of the disc-based version of the *Young Telegraph*, agrees:

> We are trying to move towards screens with hidden hot spots that do things when they are clicked on. We are trying to produce work in which the design itself encourages you to explore, and then rewards you for doing so.

She firmly believes,

> CD-Roms are not about translating text-based pages onto the screen: they are about gameplay, journeys and trying to establish a different kind of relationship between the issues and ideas presented and the gameplayer.[144]

To achieve this means abandoning the notion of the linear text, the book on a screen, and replacing it with an architectural or geographical model. The information becomes a conceptual space within which the user can wander making connections. Unfortunately, this places great responsibilities on designers. Not only do they have to design the individual screens, and the overall look and feel of the product – they also have to design the mechanisms by which the users can navigate through the conceptual space, and (crucially) retrace their steps.

It is as though designers not only have to design individual books, but also explain to the users each time what chapters, page numbers and footnotes are, and how to use them. Currently, designing digital publications often involves adopting the mantle of a teacher, trying to guide the user through an unfamiliar landscape ruled by unfamiliar laws. Using digital publications, in turn, often involves spending considerable time figuring out how they are intended to be used.

19 *Learning digitally*

In some areas, the new digital tools are being used not to create new work, but to develop means by which users can come to terms with work that has already been produced. Many libraries, galleries and educational institutions are beginning to make creative uses of the digital media in order to assist their users. Sometimes this has itself led to the construction of new work, and the establishment of new creative projects.

Chris Batt, the chief librarian at Croydon, believes that digital tools can be used to help make information and knowledge more readily obtainable. To pursue this he has established CLIP – the Croydon Libraries Internet Project – with its own full-time staff member.

CLIP has been an action research project, which has involved selecting groups of library staff and users and training them to use the Internet to search for material they would find useful. From the experience gained facilitating and monitoring these groups, CLIP has launched its own website, Croydon Online.[145] This contains a large amount of material ranging from general information about Croydon and information aimed at businesses contemplating relocating to Croydon, to a complete guide to the programmes and facilities at the Clocktower arts complex, and details of the libraries' distance learning programme, whose users have access to a suite of PCs at the main library.

Croydon Online also contains details of CLIP, and the various reports made at each stage of the project. The next stage of the project is planned to be the first step toward the creation of a *virtual community*, which 'encapsulates a vision of Croydon communicating.'[146]

Chris Batt believes that, by developing in this way, libraries can begin to segment the needs of their users, until they can 'create a virtual library for each individual user, tailored to their specific requirements'.[147] He believes that the development of the Internet makes possible the kind of learning networks that were postulated in the 1960s by educationalists such as Ivan Illich and John Holt.

This approach has been absorbed into the work of numerous galleries and museums. Many have incorporated electronic guides and experiential features into their displays. Both the Museum of the Moving Image in London and the National Museum of Photography, Film and Television in Bradford have features of this kind; but then, given the nature of their subject matter, it might be rather odd if they did not have such displays. The Science Museum in London has recently constructed a large exhibition which explores astronomy and physics by using actors and mock-ups of the Starship Enterprise, while drawing upon the entire Star Trek mythology.

Some smaller museums have also embraced this approach. The Horniman Museum in Forest Hill, South London, has a gallery containing an interactive history of music. On a series of touch-screens, users can see and hear musical instruments from different times, and from all over the world. The digitally delivered material forms a complement to the exhibits that cover the outer walls of the gallery, which consist of actual examples of the instruments.

Digital technology has proved invaluable for some institutions in helping their users to explore, and to function autonomously. Surveys[148] have shown that most people rapidly learn to use well-designed information systems, and soon become used to them. For these people the computers running the system have become as invisible as the technology which powers the telephone network.

For those charged with creating these systems, however, the technology is far from invisible. The involvement of conceptual artist Simon Poulter in digital media has led him to run training courses for other artists.

> I found that there seems to be a gap between those people who have embraced digital media and those who have continued with traditional media. Some of the people I train come because they feel a sense of anxiety about being left behind, or that their skill may be replaced by a more up-to-date method. This anxiety can quite easily be removed if creative people are given access to technology.[149]

Training for digital creativity is itself a matter of exploration. One aspect or another of the key software changes almost monthly; while the creation of interfaces, and the satisfactory organisation of content, is still a matter of argument and debate. Broadly speaking, there have been three approaches to digital training.

Firstly, there have been many self-organised initiatives, such as those in which Simon Poulter has been involved. People have come together to pool experiences and share knowledge. Sometimes, as with MacUniversity, this has resulted in the creation of a new and permanent training organisation. Richard Gooderick, the head of distribution and development at the Arts Council of England, has tried to assist this process by establishing the Hub Club, which meets monthly for showings of work, technical lectures and discussions of ideas.[150] In a similar vein, organisations such as the Institute of Contemporary Arts (ICA) have held conferences[151] around issues of aesthetics and content, in which those interested in digital creativity have had the chance to debate and discuss.

Secondly, many existing institutions of further education have begun offering courses in multimedia, which range from short courses and evening classes to two year MA courses. Of these, Newport College of Art, the University of Middlesex and the University of Westminster have become the most well known for their innovative approaches to the subject. All of them have produced CD-Roms of student work, and all of them have had students' work featured in the monthly computer press.

Thirdly, new kinds of institutions have begun to emerge to examine and teach the ideas and techniques behind digital creativity. Some of these have grown inside existing institutions, while others are entirely autonomous.

Under the editorship of Andy Cameron, The University of Westminster has established the Hypermedia Research Centre (HRC) to develop web access and 'to maximise its potential for social, artistic and technological creativity'.[152] Its intention is to create:

> the nucleus of a self-creating, self-sustaining 'virtual community' for the next generation of Internet users. Within this virtual social space, people will meet, work, learn, trade, flirt or play games with each other. The HRC will participate in the simultaneous development of the electronic marketplace and the electronic agora.[153]

To do this the Centre has, according to Simon Worthington, brought together 'an agile combination of academics, designers and artists developing innovative soft tools and bringing a synthesised visual design to Hypermedia'.[154]

Artec[155] in Islington, on the other hand, was conceived as an independent body, working in partnership with other educational and commercial organisations. It 'operates as a local, regional and national agency which works across three sectors: the arts, education and industry'.[156] It runs training courses and offers commercial services. As we have seen in the previous chapter, its clients and partners are impressive and varied.

Artec has acted as the host, or coordinator, for a number of creative initiatives, including the Media Lab which is designed to provide a programme of access and support to arts practitioners. This has taken the form of both bursaries, and support and advice sessions. Artec organised the first Internet café in England, at the ICA in March 1995, and in December 1995 became the home of the Arts Council of England's experimental Channel project, which aims to 'establish a national network of arts, photography and new media centres'[157] through activities which will include the establishment of a dedicated website.

Perhaps the most ambitious plans so far to create a free-standing environment for evolving digital creativity, however, have been hatched by Jubilee Arts,[158] in Sandwell in the West Midlands. Jubilee Arts began in 1974, and are a long-standing community arts group, who have worked increasingly with digital media in recent years. They produced *Sex Get Serious*, a multimedia presentation which won the West Midlands Regional Health of the Nation award. 'It was created by a partnership of artists, health workers and young people in Sandwell rising to the challenge of getting young people to take safe sex more seriously.'[159]

In 1995 Jubilee Arts developed detailed plans for c/Plex – a creative village to be built on seven acres of derelict land in central West Bromwich. c/Plex has been conceived as a partnership involving the local authority, arts funding organisations, the business sector and local people. It is intended that it will contain a Creative Gallery, a public square, a covered outdoor performance space and a multi-screen cinema. It is also intended to pioneer methods of digital learning, since the centre 'will have fast two-way electronic links with schools, libraries, colleges, community centres and small- to medium-sized businesses. A programme of creative and educational activities will be carried out both in the community via electronic communication and with visits to the site.'[160]

The Creative Gallery is intended to provide a programme of digital exhibitions and participatory activities. The planned range of exhibitions includes digital photography; intelligent sculpture; live Internet links with Dublin on St Patrick's Day, and Jamaica at Christmas; and exhibitions designed to link different communities in Britain electronically.

Examples of participatory activities cited in the development plans include The Bar Code Bar, which will enable visitors to 'explore unusual and unexpected uses of remote sensing technologies as well as raising issues about the control of information'[161], The Memory Bank, a living history database to which individuals and groups can add their own contributions, and Dr Wriggler's Electronic Medicine Cabinet, a multimedia health education environment.

c/Plex is an ambitious project for which Jubilee Arts are seeking funds from a variety of sources, including the National Lottery. They hope to begin work on the project in 1997 and to open it on 1 June 1999. Whether c/Plex can actually be built to this timetable, or indeed whether it can be built at all, depends largely on Jubilee's ability to raise the funds necessary. However, even if the finance is not in the end available, and the project does not therefore come to fruition, its proposal will still stand as an inspiring example of arts practitioners seeking to think through the social issues involved in the acceptance of new technology, to ensure that as many people as possible gain access to the means of digital creativity.

Digital creativity

'There are no whole truths; all truths are half-truths. It is trying to treat them as whole truths that plays the devil.'

Alfred North Whitehead

20 *State of the art*

It has been suggested that the initial content of every new medium is an old medium.[162] It takes time for the inherent potential of any new medium of expression to be understood and developed. Early movies, for example, can be seen as plays that had been filmed from the best seat in the house, with the camera remaining in a fixed position like any polite theatre-goer. The style of acting was the same expansive style that had been developed for the live performance of melodrama. It was not until the time of Sergei Eisenstein that the camera began to adopt a different position for each shot, with close-ups to emphasise drama or emotion. It was only then that film began to develop a grammar of its own, to do things that staged drama was incapable of doing. It was then that film acting and acting for the stage began to diverge.

Similarly, early television was often filmed radio, as the viewing of any episode of *The Lone Ranger* clearly demonstrates. *The Lone Ranger* was originally an American radio serial, and the television series simply continued the conventions of radio drama. Nothing ever happened on the screen without simultaneously being described verbally.

In early sound recordings, singers such as Al Jolson declaim in a booming semi-operatic style, revealing the content of the new medium to be a captured stage performance. The first popular singer to develop a style especially designed for the new medium was Bing Crosby, whose quiet conversational recording style depended on a microphone to amplify his voice sufficiently to be heard over the accompanying musicians.

Technological developments, then, have two different kinds of cultural application. They can be used to enhance an existing type of activity, as when pre-recorded music and sound effects are used in a staged drama or dance, or when television is used to broadcast the action on stage onto giant screens at large outdoor events. They can also be used to create entirely new kinds of artistic style or cultural experience, which could not obviously be produced in any other way.

Digital creativity has been used in both of these ways. Digitally created artwork appears regularly within traditional magazines: on covers, illustrating features, and in cartoons such as *Camera Obscura* in *Guardian Weekend*. Digitally created sounds are used in dance pieces, and much stage lighting is computerised. The station identification graphics on most television stations are now created digitally.

Digital creativity has also opened up the possibility of developing an entirely new medium of expression, and it is this possibility which has excited most interest among those involved. It is not surprising, though, that often this alleged new medium appears to be nothing more than a different way of presenting material from one or two older media.

Digital creativity is currently at approximately the same stage of maturity as the nascent film industry at the beginning of the silent film era. The pioneers of the silent film were not professional film-makers because there was not yet such a profession. They were hucksters, gamblers and visionaries who believed that cinema would be a popular success, and that there were fortunes to be made. The style of early films was in part determined by the fact that many early film stars had previously performed in music-hall and theatre, and carried their skills over into their films. The length of these films was mainly determined by the technical capacity of the current projectors: hence the proliferation of 'one reelers' and 'two reelers'.

In 1995, anybody with access to computing equipment costing approximately £3,000[163] could, in theory, create a professional quality CD-Rom. The style of CD-Roms is often determined by the experience their creators bring from other, older media. The size and form of the work that they produce is determined by the technical capacity of the current delivery mechanisms.

A growing band of creators are confident that the digital multimedia do represent the beginning of a new medium of expression, and that this medium will soon have its Eisenstein moment – that point at which it leaves behind its antecedents and begins to gain its own content, its own grammar and its own style. Interestingly, the consensus among those who were interviewed for this book was that, precisely because 'nobody really knows what they are doing yet', the Eisenstein moment is as likely to come from a single creator, or a small group, as from any of the currently established big international players.

Seen from the perspective of traditional 'high culture', much of the current digital material might seem banal, trivial or formulaic: the electronic equivalent of an afternoon soap opera. This is not surprising, because suspense and melodrama have always been easier to create than convincing motive and character. The popular magazines of the early twentieth century were dominated by writers like Sax Rohmer and Edgar Rice Burroughs, whose work was almost all plot-driven, with little or nothing in the way of characterisation. Popular silent films also alternated between melodrama and slapstick, but scarcely ever explored deeper waters.

It would be remarkable, then, if the beginnings of the new digital media were to be very different. People are still grappling with the possibilities of the new medium and doing what people often do in such a situation: falling back on the tried and tested, the familiar and comfortable. This is not a reason for believing that digital entertainment and digital information need be banal or, indeed, that it will always be so.

Digital creativity offers the possibility of non-linear and multi-directional narrative with all the problems which that entails. Traditionally, within the narrative arts in Europe, everything that happens contributes in one way or another to an overall moral or spiritual view. The author, the director or the composer is in sole control of the way that the narrative unfolds. In a non-linear piece there is, by definition, no single route through the material, and so the ability of the author to make dramatic points by controlling the flow of the narrative – its speed, and the juxtapositions that occur within it – is greatly diminished. Users will be free to move at their own pace, and in their own direction, through the piece. In order to explore emotional, social, moral and spiritual issues in a more sophisticated way, using non-linear digital media, it will probably be necessary to abandon the model of the author that has been developed since the eighteenth century. The creation of a navigable hypertext is, effectively, the creation of a virtual space, and thus can be seen as the work of a virtual architect.

Since the Middle Ages, architects have created spaces which are intended to evoke specific feelings and emotions within those who traverse them. The great cathedrals of Europe were designed with proportions that deliberately reminded worshippers of their puny and inconsequential stature; this humbled them and caused them to face their own insignificance. There is no single directional narrative in a medieval church, although it can sometimes be suggested by devices such as the careful placing of the depictions of the Stations of the Cross. Instead, the

space resonates everywhere with an authorial voice – however one wanders through it, and at whatever pace.

Within the digital realm that is sometimes referred to as cyberspace, it may well be that the creator will have to act as an architect in a similar way, designing virtual spaces whose very shape and contours express a view of the world, and whose landscapes encourage both thought and feelings, reflection and action in whatever direction and at whatever speed they are crossed.

21 *The information dirt-track*

If there really is to be a digital revolution, it will require at least three things. It will need a range of tools to enable work to be created digitally; it will require mechanisms to make that work easily and generally available; and it will need widespread public acceptance. At this stage, none of these factors can be taken for granted.

The tools that are currently available for digital creativity are very uneven in the state of their development. As we have seen, the tools that are used to create still images and montages are very powerful and capable of extraordinarily subtle effects. The tools that are available to musicians are also highly developed and capable of the most subtle performances. Composers have been able to move beyond the 13 semitones that comprise the standard European octave, and work easily with microtones. They have been able to move beyond conventional instruments to incorporate tuned noises into their work. Others have used synthesisers and sequencers to create work which would simply be too complex for an orchestra to learn and perform.

The huge storage capacity of CD-Roms has offered many benefits to authors, digital artists and designers, but a growing number of people believe that they are a transitionary technology. A genuine communications revolution will occur only when truly unlimited information is available. According to many people, then, it is the on-line world of the Internet that will form the keystone of any digital revolution.

There are, however, very serious problems with the Internet in its current incarnation. It has grown, through a process of accretion, from a much smaller set of networks intended for scientific and academic purposes. The original architects of the Internet never envisaged it as a public communications medium, and certainly never intended it to be the delivery mechanism for a global system of commercial traffic, cultural activity and popular entertainment.

For this reason, there is often a noticeable difference between the media hype about the wonders of global communication, and the actual experience of logging onto the Internet. Currently, for example, a single picture can take five or more minutes to appear on-screen. The speed of an Internet connection depends on three main factors: the maximum speed of your modem, the number of people sharing the same connection, and the slowest link in the chain between you and the Internet site you are connected to.

If one of the intermediate connections is running slowly, then that connection will define the maximum speed at which you will be able to send or receive information, no matter how fast your modem is. This is what causes most users' problems – and this is outside the control of anybody concerned with the Internet. The growing use of the national telephone services for activities they were never intended to cope with means that, for many people, the so-called superhighway appears more like an unmaintained dirt-track.[164]

Even when the technical mechanisms have caught up with the hyperbole, however, there will still remain problems of public acceptance. Ted Nelson envisages a world in which everything that has ever been written anywhere is available on-line, and in which everyone can add their thoughts, additions or amendments to anything that already exists. Others are understandably more cautious, but there is nonetheless widespread agreement that the costs of publishing on-line will be minimal in comparison to the costs of traditional publishing. Almost everyone who can afford the costs of going on-line will be able to afford the small additional costs involved in becoming a digital publisher.

There is a real danger that, far from increasing public acceptance of the digital realm, this will serve to put people off. If everybody makes their family albums, home movies, poems and songs available to the whole world, then it is almost certain that most people will be uninterested in most of what they find on-line most of the time.

Although we might bemoan the role of critics and reviewers, and the lack of choice available in most bookshops and record shops, it is nevertheless true that this is a process of filtering that saves many people valuable time and energy. Some form of filtering process will soon become necessary on-line. The traditional art of librarianship will remain essential, even though it may not necessarily take place within a library building.

There will be a need for people who are willing to sit for days working their way through the masses of available material on one or two subjects

– from medicine to politics and current affairs, from poetry to soap operas and original music published on-line. These people will catalogue and review this material, and publish regular on-line guides, serving a purpose similar to that of current TV listings magazines. Direct access to the whole shifting mass of unsorted material will remain possible, but most people will be content with subscribing to one or more on-line guides and following the links that they find there, while occasionally exploring at random for the same sort of reason that library users today sometimes borrow a novel they have never heard of, by an author they don't know.

Digital guides may well become essential for the widespread public acceptance of the digital realm, especially since the forms of so much that will exist there are themselves likely to be unfamiliar. Such guides are already beginning to emerge on the World Wide Web. Two American students established a database they called Yahoo,[165] which now functions as an on-line directory of thousands of different Internet sites, sponsored by advertising. By typing in keywords it is possible to find a site containing information on almost any subject.

There are a growing number of similar sites, including Mirsky's Worst, which displays a constantly updated set of links to Internet sites judged to be particularly poor, or badly designed, or simply pointless,[166] showing that one of the more obvious uses of any new medium is always humour.

22 *Build it and they will come*

Nobody can yet have any clear idea of where the digital revolution will have taken us by the turn of the century, and nobody knows what the on-line world will be like when it really works: not Bill Gates at Microsoft; not Nicholas Negroponte at MIT; not Milo Medin at @Home; and certainly not me.

International corporations are all acting in the dark, putting money into research that might – just might – give them the advantage over their competitors, despite the fact that they and their competitors have still to see any real proof that there is a realistic market for what is being developed.[167]

Everybody appears to be acting as though they were in the film *Field Of Dreams*, hearing, and believing, the siren call that whispers 'build it and they will come'. [168] This may as well be the mission statement, and business plan, of almost all those corporations currently investing in the construction of the digital revolution: that people will want it, whatever it turns out to be, for reasons they don't even question, but are in part connected to reliving the fantasies of the technologically optimistic past, when space was the place and all systems were go. Their profound hope is that magically, as in the movie, people will 'pass over the money without even thinking about it'. And they may well be proved right – for these hopes and dreams are broadly similar to those of the gamblers who set in motion the film industry, the recording industry and satellite television.

If they *are* right, and people *do* come, then the digital world will be of profound cultural importance. It will have grave effects on the ways in which other media operate, and on the ways in which they are perceived. We can be fairly certain, however, that one thing it will *not* do is to bring about the death of the book, or of the theatre or any other live arts. The death of the book might make a nice headline, but it flies in the face of history and experience. In practice, cultural forms rarely, if ever, die: they usually only exchange their temporary place at the centre of the stage for a smaller, but still culturally important, role.

The invention of photography did not, as prophesied, signal the death of painting – it merely reduced the social importance of painting, and thus somewhat altered its ranking in the public sphere. Older art forms will continue to gain support, reinventing themselves where necessary in order to do so, as opera has continued to retain a position within 'the arts', despite its high production costs and its relatively narrow appeal. Just as the *Ring Cycle* will continue to be performed, so novels and poems will continue to be written, plays will continue to be staged, and films will continue to be made. Any society that can still find a place for a cultural activity as displaced in time and space as Morris dancing is obviously reluctant to allow any art form to wither away completely.

The ways in which cultural activities, and their products, are owned and controlled are also likely to be subjected to change. Notions of copyright, and of 'intellectual property', did not exist for medieval scholars. They were evolved as a part of the development of mass-produced books, but they have begun to fray at the edges. The spread of photocopiers, tape recorders and video recorders have given most of us the ability to carry out 'criminal acts' without even thinking about it – and without actually believing that we are doing anything criminal even if we do stop to think about it.

The question of who has a right to recycle sounds and images, and who has a right to download, upload and mutate existing work, is an increasingly important one in the digital realm. This virtual space has been likened to the nineteenth-century Wild West, in which there were no laws and many people grabbed whatever they could. With this in mind, the 'Electronic Frontier Foundation was founded in July of 1990 to ensure that the principles embodied in the Constitution and Bill of Rights are protected as new communications technologies emerge.'[169]

> EFF works to make sure that common carriage principles are upheld in the information age. Common carriage principles require that network providers carry all speech, regardless of its controversial content. EFF supports a new common carriage system in which system operators are shielded from liability for the actions of users, but without the regulatory burden presently associated with common carriage ... EFF supports an Open Platform model of the global information infrastructure, providing nondiscriminatory access, based on open, private-sector standards, and free from burdensome regulation. Finally, EFF works to craft policies that enable public and private information providers to distribute and sell their information products over the

Internet. We encourage the government to provide support for schools, universities, and research labs that buy Internet services on the open market. We work on policies that encourage the government to stimulate the development of experimental, precompetitive, network technologies and to fund the development of applications that are of use to 'low-end' users, who are traditionally underserved by advanced digital media.[170]

The EFF have raised funds to fight numerous legal battles in the USA in order to prevent the possibilities of the new media being crushed beneath the weight of tradition. They are doing this precisely because they acknowledge that 'nobody knows what they are doing yet'. They argue that cyberspace is (or is akin to) newly discovered territory, and that it should not be colonised by corporations and governments using rules developed for entirely different circumstances.

The very existence of the EFF should serve to remind us that digital creativity is much more of a cultural and political issue than a matter of technical specification. The exploration of cyberspace (should it turn out, in the end, to be explorable) will not be a job for computers. It will be a task for creative human beings, using computers as powerful tools to make new kinds of work from which we can derive meaning.

23 *The world tomorrow*

One of the enduring arguments about the nature of culture in the twentieth century has concerned what has been termed 'the ownership of the means of cultural production'. It has been argued that one of the consequences of the industrial revolution was that culture ceased to be a mutual and social activity, and became just another centrally manufactured product for mass consumption.

Public culture traditionally involved complex processes of social interaction, and it has been suggested that this interactivity largely disappeared in the early twentieth century. Whereas the audiences at theatres had for centuries given vent to their feelings – demanding encores or booing unsuccessful performers off the stage – cheering and booing at the cinema was soon recognised as a pointless activity that could have no possible effect on the performance on the screen. When the cinema itself began to be eclipsed by television and video, much 'public' entertainment took place at home and the possibilities of audience interaction further dwindled.

The more gung-ho advocates of the Internet make great play of the possibilities it presents for reintroducing interactivity to cultural life. This argument takes one of two forms. Firstly, it is suggested,

> somewhere between a book, a TV show and a penny arcade, the hypertext can be a vast tapestry of information all in plain English (spiced with a few magic tricks on the screen), which the reader may attack and play for the things he wants, branching and jumping on the screen, using simple controls as though he were driving a car.[171]

It is argued that as people create their own trails through the digital space of hypertext, they will literally be engaged in an act of creativity – making their own unique links through logic and rationality, but also through allusion and imaginative leaps. People will create their own unique dataspheres which reveal and reflect aspects of their creators' natures, as any creative work does.

Secondly, it is argued that the Internet will be truly interactive in that every reader can become an author, because every receiver is also capable of being a transmitter. It is suggested that the Internet will be the start of a gigantic communal project in which culture ceases to be made by the few for the many and becomes instead a collective democratic enterprise. While this is undoubtedly possible in principle, there are reasons to be sceptical about the likelihood of the sudden flowering of a billion electronic authors, each with their own authentic tales to tell, and each capable of capturing our attention.

This argument has been proposed many times this century with regard to different technological breakthroughs, and it has never yet proved true. Popular new activities have resulted from technical developments but the control of culture has still failed to become democratised. Millions of snapshots are taken each year by millions of ordinary people, for example, but the images that fill magazines, television-screens and public spaces are still all the work of highly-paid professional photographers. Family albums have by and large remained private.

Technological optimists made similar claims for the democratising potential of both the video camera and the cheap offset litho printing presses that appeared in the 1970s. In retrospect, it is true that these technologies made certain new forms of communication possible, but their effectiveness always depended on the strength of the content that was being communicated.

In the early 1980s, similar claims were advanced for the ability of the new portastudios[172] to democratise the music industry, if not render it completely redundant. For two years the leading weekly rock magazines devoted at least a page a week to brief reviews and contact addresses for tapes made at home. This movement floundered because of the decidedly uneven quality of the tapes. Widespread access to cheap recording equipment proved no guarantee that very much of public interest would emerge.

There is one important area, however, in which the nature of the Internet may enable wider groups of people to make their ideas and images public. Material on the Internet is essentially anonymous, and therefore all has the same effective status. Where material *is* signed there is currently no way of verifying the signature. On-line communication is therefore fluid and malleable. It allows people to try on different identities, and to discover some of the consequences of wearing them. This may allow people to take control of the means by which they project themselves culturally in a way that has not previously been possible.

Many people believe that this fluidity could make the digital world into a space that is less inherently disadvantageous for women and ethnic minorities. Some, like computer programmer and on-line activist Jude Milhon, would go further and assert that 'girls *need* modems.'[173]

The fluidity of the on-line world, and the sense of communal experimentation, will almost certainly prove temporary. In course of time the new medium will become weighed down by preconceptions and expectations, by standards and commercially ordained formats, just as all previous media have. Eventually there will be new digital professions, with their own career paths, and their own equivalent of Oscars and the Turner Prize. For the moment, however, the nature of these standards and formats is still in the balance. It is impossible to predict what the digital future will turn out to be.

Those pessimists who like to refer to themselves as realists say that it will be imposed by a very small number of large-scale participants, while the digital optimists argue that it will be built organically by a very large number of small-scale participants. In the former case, we can look forward to a digital realm that mimics the format of the industrial mass media: a global web dominated by a few corporations whose idea of interactivity is to offer a limited range of personally customisable packages for subscribers. The latter case is the one proposed by long-time Internet users, and by organisations such as the Electronic Frontier Foundation: a digital culture which is democratically organised, and in which everybody is welcome.

The likelihood, of course, is that in practice the future will be nowhere near as neatly packaged as this. The precedents described earlier make it seem exceedingly unlikely that culture will become democratised to the point where everybody is a digital creator and the profession of artist disappears. On the other hand, the growth of relatively cheap digital tools, and the simultaneous development of cheap methods of distribution make it likely that there will be a dramatic growth in the amount and range of cultural material available, and in the kinds of people producing it.

The work of commercially published creators and officially sanctioned artists may become less important to many people as they realise that, increasingly, the interesting work is not necessarily where you might expect it to be.[174] The differences between commercial and non-commercial work, between 'serious' and 'popular' material, have become very blurred in the digital realm. The boundaries between the traditionally different art forms have, in some cases, disappeared completely.

This can either be seen as an opportunity, or as a threat. Fortunately many creative people are choosing to see it as an opportunity. They are enhancing their work in the traditional media and, in some cases, they are embarking upon the challenging task of helping to construct entirely new media.

Notes

1 The electronic publications mentioned in this paragraph are all websites – a term which is fully explained in Chapter 7. Their addresses are:
Electronic Telegraph: http://www.telegraph co.uk
Guardian GO2:   http://go2.guardian.co.uk/
New Scientist: http://www.newscientist.com
SoccerNet: http://www..soccernet.com
Time Out: http://www.timeout.com

2 This promise was made in a speech at the 1995 Labour Party conference.

3 There are other important reasons for maintaining a wide definition of 'the arts'. Primary among these is the fact that the activities that are deemed to comprise 'the arts' change over time, according to the nature and purposes of the people doing the defining.

4 Babbage did not, of course, develop his ideas out of thin air. He intended using a technique which had already been developed successfully in the textile industry, where the Jacquard loom used punched cards to vary its patterns.

5 *Out of Control: the new biology of machines* by Kevin Kelly (Addison Wesley, 1994).

6 Kelly, ibid.

7 Kelly, ibid.

8 A computer screen is composed of a grid of tiny dots, or pixels. A 14-inch Macintosh screen contains a grid of 640 x 480 pixels: a total of 307,200 dots. If a movie used a palette of just 256 colours, then each pixel would need to be described by an eight-bit 'word'. (This is because of the nature of binary numbers, which is discussed in a footnote in Chapter 4. Put simply, there are 256 possible combinations of noughts and ones in a vocabulary composed of binary 'words' which are each eight digits long.) If full motion animation requires 24 frames a second, then the computer would have to transfer 58,982,400 bits of information from a CD-ROM to its processors and then onto the screen every second that the movie played. This is a transfer rate well in excess of the capabilities of the current generation of desktop computers.

9 *Very Spaghetti: the potential of interactive multimedia in art galleries*. Reports by Richard Francis, Colin Grigg, Sandy Nairne, Isobel Pring, (Arts Council, 1992).

10 *Starship Traveller* by Steve Jackson (Puffin, 1983).

11 Jackson, ibid.

12 ASCII used seven bits for each character. A bit is the smallest unit of information a computer is capable of recognising. It is either a 0 or a 1. Putting seven bits together gives 'words' ranging from 0000000 to 1111111. There are 128 possible combinations of 0s and 1s. Later, to double the number of characters, an eighth bit was used.

(The principle of binary code isn't difficult to understand. In our normal decimal system there are 10 numbers: 0 to 9. In binary number systems there are only 2 numbers: 0 and 1. When we run out of numbers in the decimal system we add another column to the left and start the right-hand column again at nought, so that 9 plus 1 is written as 10. In binary systems the same idea applies, except of course we run out of numbers almost straight away. So, in a binary system,1 plus 1 is written as 10, 1 plus 2 is written as 11, and 1 plus 3 is written as 100.

Why would anyone invent such a bizarre system when we already have a perfectly good set of numbers? The answer is that if you have a number system that has only 2 digits in it you can use it to count in a machine that has only 2 states – switched on and switched off – by having the machine recognise 0 as 'off' and 1 as 'on'. That is the basis of everything that computers do. They do everything by counting in binary numbers, and they produce the effects they produce, from games to music, because they count very very quickly. In a computer there are millions of these switching processes, each of which can switch from 'on' to 'off' millions of times per second.

13 The Internet addressing system works by common agreement, and has a standard format. In this format each computer that is connected to the Internet is referred to as a node. Each node has its own unique IP address, so that it can be distinguished from every other node. IP addresses consist of four bytes of data: that is, they are groups of four 8-digit binary 'words' such as 01010101.

There are 256 possible 'words' in an 8-bit 'language', which can be written as the numbers from 0 to 255. An Internet address will therefore look something like this: 245.233.123.8, or this: 23.56.77.214.

To make the Internet easier to use each address is assigned a name, using an agreed protocol called the Domain Name System. These names are referred to as domain names, and provide the more usual way of addressing people using electronic mail. They look something like this: owenk@booha.easynet.co.uk

When e-mail is sent using an address like this, software on the Internet called Domain Name servers translates the domain name into the actual IP address that the Internet itself uses. This is a communal (and therefore inevitably somewhat *ad hoc*) way of providing an interface which is reasonably easy to use.

Domain names are not difficult to understand, and provide information about the location of the person to whom you are sending messages, or the location of the computer that you are accessing. The part of the address to the left of the @ symbol is the person's personal mailbox, and it is located at the place (or more accurately the domain) indicated by that part of the address to the right of the @ symbol.

In the case of the example above, which is my e-mail address, the domain is Easynet, an Internet service provider based in London. The **co** indicates that this domain is a commercial organisation. If it had been a university it would have said **uni** or **ac**; if it had been a voluntary organisation it would have said **org**. The **uk** part indicates the country in which it is located. Since the Internet has been primarily an American development, nodes in the USA do not normally bother to put **usa** at the end of their domain name. Nodes in other countries do, however, need this final part of the address.

Almost all domain names are in lower case letters, for technical reasons concerning the Unix operating system used by most large university and research computers.

14 Hypertext refers to an approach to storing, sorting and accessing data. It begins from the premise that data in a computer can be ordered and accessed in any order and according to any number of criteria. Pools of data could be built

through which users could swim in different directions and to different depths, according to their needs.

An indication of how this can be achieved is given in the discussion of HyperCard later.

15 *Dream Machines*, p.5 (Microsoft Press, 1987 ed).

16 *Dream Machines*, p.143 (Microsoft Press, 1987 ed).

17 I have tried to make the description that follows short and clear. In doing so I have oversimplified some things to the point of making them technically inaccurate.

For those who wish to know, HyperTalk is almost, but not quite, an object-orientated language. If you want a long but accurate account of HyperCard, read *The Complete HyperCard Handbook* by Danny Goodman (Bantam Books, 1987). If you want to know everything there is to know about HyperTalk read *HyperTalk: The Book* by Dan Winkler and Scott Kamins (Bantam Books, 1990). Dan Winkler created HyperTalk.

18 Other programs include Allegiant's SuperCard on the Apple Macintosh, and Assymetric's Toolbox on IBM-compatible PCs. In addition, Macromedia's Director is a powerful animation program which is capable of creating hypertext links. It works on both Macintoshes and PCs.

19 The islands and landscapes that form part of the interface on the CD-Rom that accompanies this book were built using Bryce.

20 These are just two of the many games on many different games machines that could have served as examples. *Super Mario Kart* is particularly noteworthy for its cute graphics, lack of violence, compulsive playability, immense detail, and astonishing texture mapping. The opening of each race, in which the 'camera' zooms into a front view of the character you are playing and then pans round to give you a view from behind the car is particularly impressive.

21 *Mondo 2000: a user's guide to the new edge*, Rudy Rucker, R U Sirius and Queen Mu eds. (HarperPerennial, 1992).

22 *Edge*, issue 3, December 1993.

23 From *Fire in the Valley* by Michael Goldberg – *Wired* 2.01 (US edition) January 1994.

24 You can reach Worlds Inc, and download the special software you need to take part in their experimental worlds, by contacting their Website at http://www.worlds.net

25 *Virtual Intercourse*, by Jim McClellan, in Cyberspace, *Observer Life*, 10 December 1995.

26 *The Real Frank Zappa Book*, by Frank Zappa with Peter Occhiogrosso, p.161 (Poseidon Press, 1989).

27 This title was derived from the fictitious group locked in eternal opposition to the Illuminati in Robert Anton Wilson and Robert Shea's *Illuminatus* trilogy.

28 *Justified and Ancient History*, p.7, by Pete Robinson (self published, 1993).

29 *Justified and Ancient History*, p.9, by Pete Robinson.

30 The JAMs renamed themselves the KLF (Kopyright Liberation Front) shortly after this event, and proceeded to have a number of international hit records. After *Justified and Ancient*, with vocals by Tammy Wynette, reached number two in the charts, they disbanded. They re-emerged later as The K Foundation – the 'art pranksters' who awarded Rachael Whitehead £40,000 for being the worst artist in Britain at the 1994 Turner Prize, and then subsequently filmed themselves burning £1,000,000. They then showed this film at various betting shops while trying to instigate a debate about the nature of value.

31 Reprinted in *Musicworks* magazine, no. 34, spring 1986.

32   *The Man Who Stole Michael Jackson's Face* by David Gans, from *Wired* 3.02, February 1995.

33   Gans, ibid.

34   Phil Lesh is the Grateful Dead's bassist, and a keen enthusiast of modern classical music. It was at his instigation that the Grateful Dead established the Rex Foundation, in honour of a roadie who was killed in an accident. The Rex Foundation has no application forms, or programmes of funding. Instead it awards grants to composers on its own initiative, and with no strings attached. Robert Simpson is among the British composers who have benefited from awards from the Rex Foundation.

35   George Clinton is regarded by many as second in importance only to James Brown in terms of the development of Black American funk music. He was the leader of Funkadelic and Parliament, whose ground-breaking albums such as *Mothership Connection, One Nation Under A Groove, Motor-Booty Affair*, and *Uncle Jam Wants You* were huge successes in the 1970s. He has since released influential recordings such as *Atomic Dog* and *Loopzilla*, while continuing to tour and record with the P-Funk All Stars.

36   The licensing notes in the package state that 'we will NOT charge you or your record company any up-front flat fee for the use of the sample(s), instead you or your record company will pay on each record sold'. The fees vary according to whether the sample used contains the full band, a 'breakdown' of just two or three instruments, or drums or a single instrument.

37   From *One 2 One* by William Shoebridge, *Mute*, issue 1.

38   Brian Eno *Discreet Music* (Editions EG/Obscure, 1975).

39   *Brian Eno: his music and the vertical color of sound* by Eric Tamm (Faber & Faber, 1989).

40   Fripp and Eno released two recordings: (*No Pussyfooting*) (Editions EG, 1973) and *Evening Star* (Editions EG, 1975). Using similar techniques (which he termed frippertronics) Robert Fripp made *Let The Power Fall* (Editions EG, 1981), an album of live performances.

41   From the liner notes of Robert Fripp's *1999* (Discipline GM, 1995).

42   From the liner notes of Robert Fripp's *1999* (Discipline GM, 1995).

43   In this specific sense some ambient dub *does* work as ambient music. The KLF's compact disc *Chill Out* (KLF Communications, 1990), for example, is a sound collage rather than a piece of music, and is designed to provide the quiet rooms at the end of a rave with a slowly shifting atmosphere.

44   Hence recordings such as *Ambient 1: Music For Airports* (Editions EG, 1979).

45   From David Jackson's publicity material, summer 1995.

46   Soundbeam is manufactured by The Soundbeam Project, Unit 3, Highbury Villas, St Michael's Way, Bristol BS2 8BY. You can e-mail them at 100530.3530@CompuServe.com

47   From David Jackson's publicity material, summer 1995.

48   From David Jackson's publicity material, summer 1995.

49   From the liner notes of *Diagonal Flying* by Rolf Gehlhaar and Roger Woodward (Etcetera Records, 1992). This record contains four of Gehlhaar's pieces, as performed at the Second Sydney International Festival of New Music. Three of the pieces are compositions from the 1970s, using tape delay. The final piece *Diagonal Flying* is a duet for piano and 'Sound-Space'.

50   From a conversation with Rolf Gehlhaar.

51   From the liner notes of *Diagonal Flying* by Rolf Gehlhaar and Roger Woodward (Etcetera Records, 1992).

52   From the liner notes of *Diagonal Flying* by Rolf Gehlhaar and Roger Woodward

(Etcetera Records, 1992).

53   Strictly speaking, this is not completely true, in so far as two beams will feed back on each other if they intersect. However, this intersection will merely cause each of the beams to separately act as though they were being interrupted. It will not cause any additional effects to occur.

54   From a conversation with Rolf Gehlhaar.

55   From a conversation with Rolf Gehlhaar.

56   *Musical Madness – the Cyber-tribal D'Cuckoo* by Leah Lin, *Axcess*, vol. II, no 3.

57   You can contact D'Cuckoo at dcuckoo@well.sf.ca.us

58   D'Cuckoo in conversation with R U Sirius and Jas Morgan, *Mondo 2000*, issue 4.

59   Lin, ibid.

60   Lin, ibid.

61   From *The Legible City* by Jeffrey Shaw, *Ten•8*, vol. 2, no. 2, 1991.

62   From *The Conquest of Form: computer art* by William Latham (Arnolfini Gallery, 1988).

63   Latham, ibid.

64   Latham, ibid.

65   Latham, ibid.

66   From a talk following *Unearthly Delights – the computer art of William Latham*, part of the Digital Underground season, the National Film Theatre, 20 April 1995.

67   Latham, ibid.

68   From *Sacred Geometry* by Robert Lawlor (Thames & Hudson, 1982).

69   From *The Pattern Book: Fractals in Art and Nature*, Clifford A Pickover ed., p.v, (World Scientific, 1995).

70   *The Fractal Geometry of Nature* by Benoît Mandelbrot (WH Freeman & Company, 1985).

71   The procedure used to generate a Mandelbrot set is not, in principle, complex. As described by Benjamin Woolley, in his book *Virtual Worlds* (Penguin, 1992), 'you take a number, square it, square the result and add the number you started with, square that result and add the number you started with and so on'.

72   *From Fractals (Endlessly Repeated Geometrical Figures)* by Hans Lauwerier (Princeton University Press, 1991).

73   The thirteenth-century Italian mathematician Fibonacci (Leonardo of Pisa) first drew attention to the sequence beginning 1, 1 in which every succeeding number is producing by adding the two preceding numbers: 1, 1, 2, 3, 5, 8, 13, 21, 34 and so on. In the last 30 years this series has been found to apply to a number of widely differing phenomena including the branch structure of many trees, the organisation of bees in a hive and the fecundity of rabbits. It also has applications in psychology and astronomy.

74   From *Sacred Geometry* by Robert Lawlor (Thames & Hudson, 1982).

75   From a talk following *Unearthly Delights – the computer art of William Latham*, part of the Digital Underground season, the National Film Theatre, 20 April 1995.

76   *When is Seeing Believing* by William J Mitchell, *Scientific American* special issue: the computer in the 21st century, January 1995.

77   See, for example, *Truth, Justice and the new Photo (shop) Realism* by Jacques Leslie in *Wired* 1.02 UK edn, May 1995.

78   *When is Seeing Believing* by William J Mitchell, *Scientific American* special issue: the computer in the 21st century, January 1995.

79   A simple example of photographic manipulation comes with the choice of lens

a photographer makes. The typical appearance of a snapshot is due, in large part, to the fact that most cheap cameras have a lens of approximately 50mm, whereas most professional photographers use a whole range of different lenses. A £50 camera is mechanically incapable of producing the kind of photograph that sports photographers produce.

80   From *Digital Memories* by Trisha Ziff, *Ten•8*, vol. 2, no. 2, 1991.

81   The Original Photograph Club has published a booklet of the images in Daniel Lee's Judgement series (vol. 2, no. 1, 1995). In this series the various people each represent a member of the jury that Buddhist mythology says will judge creatures after their death. Each figure is drawn from an animal or spirit in Chinese mythology.

82   From *Manimal Farm* by Sue Weekes in *Creative Technology*, May 1995.

83   From *Manimal Farm* by Sue Weekes in *Creative Technology*, May 1995.

84   From a conversation with Pete Dunn.

85   *Digital Vision in Docklands* from *20/20*, the national magazine for photography and media education, issue 3, autumn 1995.

86   *Digital Vision in Docklands* from *20/20*, issue 3, Autumn 1995.

87   From *The Photoshop Wow! Book* by Linnea Dayton and Jack Davis (Peachpit Press, 1993).

88   Advertisement in *Wired* 2.05 US edition, May 1994.

89   You can find the Virtual Library museums page at: http://www.comlab.ox.ac.uk /archive/other/museums.html

90   You can visit Le WebMuseum at http://mistral.enst.fr/wm/net

91   It opened under the name LeWebLouvre, but was forced to change its name by the French Ministry of Culture.

92   You can visit the Natural History Museum at http://www.nhm.ac.uk

93   From *The Future of History* by Tom Standage, in *.net* issue 5, April 1995.

94   From *The Future of History* by Tom Standage, in *.net* issue 5, April 1995.

95   From conversations with Terry Braun.

96   You can visit the Rhombus Gallery at http://www.cybermalls.com/rhombus/index.html

97   From *Developing the art of easy access* by Wendy Grossman in *Guardian Online*, 15 June 1995.

98   You can visit the Genetic Art II project at http://robocop.modmath.cs.cmu.edu:8001/ where you can help vote the next generation of images into existence.

99   You can visit the Digital Research Centre at http://dougal.derby.ac.uk/gallery/

100 From *Picture the Future* by Ivan Pope, in .net, issue 5, April 1995.

101 You can visit the Pavilion Internet Gallery on http://www.pavilion.co.uk

102 You can visit The Place at http://gertrude.art.uiuc.edu/ludgate/the/place/html

103 From *Multidisciplinary Dweeb* by Burr Snider, in *Wired* 2.02, US edition, February 1994.

104 From *Multidisciplinary Dweeb* by Burr Snider, in *Wired* 2.02, US edition, February 1994.

105 From *Multidisciplinary Dweeb* by Burr Snider, in *Wired* 2.02, US edition, February 1994.

106 From *Multidisciplinary Dweeb* by Burr Snider, in *Wired* 2.02, US edition, February 1994.

107 From a conversation with Nicola Triscott and Vivienne Glance.

108 From a conversation with Nicola Triscott and Vivienne Glance.

109 From *Connections!* issue 7, August 1995.

110 From *Computer Vision* by Duncan Gillies, in *The Nature of History* catalogue

(Film and Video Umbrella, 1995).

111   From the transcript of a talk by Simon Poulter.

112   From *Simon Poulter – UK Ltd in Propaganda?* a programme of newly commissioned live art in Hull (Hull Time Based Arts, 1995).

113   From an interview with Simon Poulter.

114   From the transcript of a talk by Simon Poulter.

115   From the introductory notes to the Laboratory's website at http://www.ruskin-sch.ox.ac.uk/

116   You can reach *The Cooker* at http://www.ruskin-sch.ox.ac.uk/~jake/tilson.html

117   Simon Biggs' website is at http://www.easynet.co.uk/simonbiggs/

118   From *Knowledge of Angels* by Jim McClellan in *Observer Life*, 24 March 1996.

119   Simon Biggs' work is illustrated in a book and CD-Rom *Book Of Shadows* (Ellipsis, 1996).

120   There were similar attempts to break away from a single fixed point of view within painting, another fi d which requires comparatively little in the way of equipment. Partly this is because of the encroachment of photography onto much of the traditional territory of painting. Landscapes and portraits could now be rendered mechanically with complete 'realism'. The result of this was that mere craft no longer seemed sufficient. Salvador Dalí wrote: 'What must one think of a man who spent all his life trying to paint round apples, and who never succeeded in painting anything but convex apples?... One has to be extremely awkward to be content with painting apples that are such a failure that they cannot even be eaten. Dalí declares that Cézanne is only a bricklayer.'

        Much painting at the beginning of the century attempted to deal with this problem. Sometimes, as with Dalí, the solution was to paint the fantastic – scenes which had no literal reference in real life. Sometimes the solution was to attempt to present the viewer with simultaneous multiple viewpoints. Marcel Duchamp's *Nude Descending a Staircase* provides a powerful example of this approach.

121   *Dada: art and anti-art* by Hans Richter (Thames & Hudson, 1965).

122   Richter, ibid.

123   Richter, ibid.

124   *Coincidance* by Robert Anton Wilson (Falcon Press, 1991).

125   Quoted in *Coincidance* by Robert Anton Wilson (Falcon Press, 1991).

126   *A William Burroughs Reader*, edited by John Calder (Picador, 1986).

127   *A novel use for the computer* by Steve Johnson, in *Guardian Online*, 29 September 1994.

128   *A novel use for the computer* by Steve Johnson, in *Guardian Online*, 29 September 1994.

129   The address of The Spot is http://www.thespot.com/

130   The characters are played by actors or models, and their photographs illustrate the various narratives. For those who feel they need to know this, because it might be in a future edition of Trivial Pursuit, the original characters were Tara Hartwick, Carrie Seaver, Michelle Foster, Lon Oliver and Jeff Beaton. Tomeiko Pierce and Audrey Fairweather were added later.

131   From a meeting with Andreas and Ben Whittam Smith.

132   From *Patrician enters a new world* by Nick Rosen, in *Guardian Online*, 14 December 1995.

133   From *Blood on the Streets* by Tony Feldman in *Interactive Media International*, vol. 9, no. 11.

134   Simply put, this means that what is transmitted over the Internet is securely

encoded, and will appear as utter gibberish unless it is 'unlocked' with the right PIN number.

The arguments concerning the inviolability of encryption are technical and complex, and outside the scope of this book. There seems to be a growing willingness, however, for large companies to consider offering home shopping over the Internet, in which payment is made through credit card details sent over the Internet. Barclays have recently launched BarclaySquare, which is intended to be a fully fledged 'virtual shopping mall'.

135 You can visit *HotWired* at http://www.wired.com/
136 From *Interactive Media International* newsletter, vol. 9, no. 12, December 1995.
137 There are probably literally thousands of webzines currently being published to varying degrees of public attention. The following are the addresses (as of December 1995) of a few which are worth looking at:

Brainstorm	http://www.well.com/user/hlr/
Caketimes	http://itrc.on.ca/caketimes
Fix	http://www.easynet.co.uk/fix/contents.html
Sense	http://www.virtual.co.uk/sense
Zug	http:/www.xensil.com:80/users/zug/about/about.html

138 You can visit the electronic *bOING bOING* at http://www.well.com/user/mark although this address may change. You can find out the current address by e-mailing Carla Sinclair at carla@well.com
139 E-mail interview with Mark Frauenfelder.
140 You can visit *Rebel Inc* at http://www.electricfrog.co.uk/rebelinc/
141 Interview with Frank Boyd.
142 Interview with Terry Braun.
143 Interview with Philip Ellington.
144 Interview with Caroline Grimshaw.
145 You can visit Croydon Online at: http://www.croydon.gov.uk
146 From the Clip 2 report, July 1995.
147 Interview with Chris Batt.
148 In 1993, Surrey County Council pioneered the development of a town information plan using Reigate and Redhill as a case study. This was initiated and coordinated by the County Libraries and Leisure Service, under the leadership of John Saunders, the County Director of Libraries. There was already an interactive information service available in the main libraries. During the course of the research a number of detailed surveys were carried out to determine the reaction of a range of users to the technology.
149 From the transcript of a talk by Simon Poulter.
150 The Hub Club has a website as well as monthly meetings in London and Bristol. You can visit the website at: http://www.ace.mdx.ac.uk/Hub/Hub.html
151 These have included *4 Acres and a Microchip*, held in June 1995, which moved beyond questions of aesthetics to address the key issue of representation in cyberspace, by examining issues surrounding the access of people of colour to the digital domain.
152 This mission statement is set out on the HRC website, which you can visit at http://www.hrc.wmin.ac.uk/
153 From the HRC website, which you can visit at http://www.hrc.wmin.ac.uk/
154 From *404URL not found* by Simon Worthington in *Mute*, issue 3, autumn 1995.
155 For more information about Artec you can e-mail info@artec.gn.apc.org
156 From *Interface*, issue 2, June 1995.
157 From *Interface*, issue 2, June 1995.
158 You can contact Jubilee Arts by e-mailing sylvia@jubart.demon.co.uk

159 Publicity leaflet for *Sex Get Serious*.

160 From Jubilee Arts' National Lottery application form for the c/Plex project.

161 From Jubilee Arts' National Lottery application form for the c/Plex project.

162 *Understanding Media* by Marshall McLuhan (Routledge and Kegan Paul, 1964).

163 A reasonably fast Macintosh or PC with at least 20 megabytes of RAM; a desktop scanner; a camcorder; a microphone and tape deck; and a 1-gigabyte hard disk. And the relevant software, which probably includes (at least) Adobe Photoshop, Adobe Premiere, Macromedia SoundEdit 16, and either Macromedia Director or Allegiant SuperCard...

164 A radical solution is being proposed by a number of cable companies, who are suggesting that the Internet could soon bypass the telephone system altogether. The coaxial cable used for most cable television is capable of carrying digital signals at up to 700 times the speed of the most popular modems attached to a phone line. The US cable company Tele-Communications Inc. is so confident of this approach that it has formed a separate company @Home to develop this, and has hired Milo Medin, the man who developed the original IP protocol which forms the basis of the Internet, to lead it.

165 You can contact Yahoo at http://www.yahoo.com/

166 You can contact Mirsky's Worst at http://mirsky.turnpike.net/wow/Worst.html

167 It is interesting, in this context, to note that a recent, and largely unpublicised, trial of BT's proposed interactive television service, which was supposed to demonstrate the advantages of home shopping, home banking and video on demand, has apparently failed to ignite the imaginations of many of those who participated. Some people found the services disappointing, while others found that the custom-built service suffered from the same problems as the Internet – it slowed down, became temporarily unavailable or simply didn't work in the ways that they wanted.

  See *Video off demand*, by Azeem Azhar in *Guardian Online*, 18 January 1996.

168 *Field Of Dreams*, written and directed by Phil Alden Robinson, 1990.

169 From *All About the Electronic Frontier Foundation*, a paper available from the EFF's website, which is at http://www.eff.org

170 EFF, ibid.

171 *Dream Machines* by Ted Nelson (Microsoft Press, 1987).

172 Portastudios were (and still are) multitrack tape recorders that use ordinary high quality cassette tape to produce recordings of professional quality. Often costing less than £500, they are capable of at least matching the standard of recording equipment that the Beatles used to record *Sgt. Pepper*.

173 Jude Milhon is more usually known on-line as St Jude, and under this name she has spent more than a decade fighting for radical causes on-line.

  From *Modem Grrrl*, an interview by Rosie Cross in *Wired* 3.02, US edition, February 1995.

174 The 'conceptual artist' Heath Bunting's website (which is idiosyncratic, but invariably interesting) is a salutary reminder that, in the digital revolution, the interesting stuff won't necessarily come from where you expect it.

  Heath Bunting can be found (from time to time) at http://www.cybercafe.org/cybercafe/ and, in my opinion, it's well worth checking this site out regularly.

  He has recently launched a new website PAIN OF EXISTANCE (sic) which can be found at http://www.irrational.org/pain

Index

Absolut Museum 73
Adobe Photoshop 67
Altair 8800 16
Apple 16
Art of Change 70-71
Artec 93, 99-100
Arts Catalyst 78-79
ASCII 27
Babbage, Charles 15
Ball, Hugo 82
Batt, Chris 97
Biggs, Simon 81
bOING bOING 91
Boyd, Frank 93
Braun, Terry 74, 94
Burroughs, William 84
Cameron, Andy 99
Cliggett, Jack 71
Clinton, George 51
CLIP 97
Concept 3 Advertising 71
Crosby, Bing 105
D'Cuckoo 60
Daily Mail 9
Daily Mirror 19
Daily Telegraph 9
DARPANET 33
Dick, Philip K 17
Dunn, Pete 70
Electronic Frontier Foundation
    113-114
Ellington, Philip 95
ENIAC 15
Eno, Brian 53-54
Esperanto 26
Feldman, Tony 89
Fibonacci series 66
Francis, Richard 22
Frauenfelder, Mark 91
Fripp, Robert 54
Gehlhaar, Rolf 58-60
Genetic Art Gallery 75
Goldberg, Diego 68
Gooderick, Richard 99
Grimshaw, Caroline 96
Guardian Online 9
Gutenberg, Johann 19
Hawkins, Spike 84
Holzer, Jenny 77-78
Horniman Museum 98
HotWired 90
HTML 36
HUB Club 99
HyperCard 37-39
Internet 33-34

Jackson, David 55-57
Jackson, Steve 24
JAMs 48
Johnson, BS 84-85
Joyce, James 83
Joyce, Michael 85
Jubilee Arts 99-100
jukebox 19
Kelly, Kevin 17
KidPix 67
Lamsweerde, Inez van 69-70
Latham, William 63-65
Leary, Timothy 11
Lee, Daniel 69
Leeson, Lorraine 70
MacUniversity 95
Mandelbrot, Benoît 65
MIDI 31
Moog, Robert 29 -30
Natural History Museum 74
Negroponte, Nicholas 9
Nelson, Ted 36, 110
New Scientist 9
Orb 51
Oswald, John 49
Paul, Les 29
Pavilion 76
plunderphonics 49-50
Poulter, Simon 79-80, 98
radio broadcasting 19
ray-tracing 41
Rebel Inc. 91
Rhodes, Joseph 26
Rhombus Gallery 75
Scanner 51
Shaw, Jeffrey 62
Sinclair, Carla 91
Small, Peter 88
Smith, Andreas Whittam 88
The Lone Ranger 105
The Spot 86
Tilson, Jake 80-81
Time Out 9
Times 9
Toffler, Alvin 9
Tzara, Tristan 84
University of Derby 75
Virtuality 42
VRML 43
Williamson, Kevin 91
Wilson, Robert Anton 83
Worlds Inc. 43
Xerox PARC 16
Yahoo 111
Zappa, Frank 47